♦ ♦ ♦

Silent Cal's Almanack:
The Homespun Wit and Wisdom of Vermont's Calvin Coolidge

♦ ♦ ♦

Edited by
David Pietrusza

a createspace book

D0369553

Silent Cal's Almanack:
The Homespun
Wit and Wisdom of
Vermont's Calvin Coolidge

To
Jim Cooke

© 2008, 2010, 2011 David Pietrusza. All rights reserved. Printed in the United States of America. No part of this book may be used or reproduced in any manner whatsoever without written permission except in the case of brief quotations embodied in critical articles and reviews.

For information email: dap@davidpietrusza.com.

ISBN: 1438245408
EAN-13: 9781438245409

www.davidpietrusza.com

www.createspace.com

10 9 8 7 6 5 4 3 2

3-03-11

Contents

Why Silent Cal?

The question before us: Why chronicle and commemorate the words of the wordless Calvin Coolidge, a politician and president renowned for doing nothing and saying less?

Because the basic premise of the question is doubly flawed.

The modern world views Silent Cal Coolidge as a failure, a political and personal cipher, a man who not only accomplished nothing, but who, as columnist and pundit Walter Lippmann famously charged, possessed a veritable "genius for inactivity."

It all depends, of course, on how one deigns to define "inactivity." Presumably, Mr. Lippmann meant to damn Coolidge as an unimaginative, listless leader. And that is certainly bad. But, if "inactivity" is defined as a spirited, principled, often brilliantly eloquent, *active* opposition to government intervention in the economy and the invariably crushing tax burdens that follow—that is profoundly good, and, in articulating and implementing that opposition Calvin Coolidge was most decidedly a "genius."

Coolidge did not, of course, view himself as either a genius or a great man "It is," he observed, "a great advantage to a President, and a major source of safety to the country, for him to know he is not a great man." But Calvin Coolidge did possess a remarkably coherent philosophy of government—and of life itself. In fact, historian Paul Johnson has praised this supposed cipher as "the most internally consistent and single-minded of modern American presidents."

Calvin Coolidge may have indeed been the last Jeffersonian, a man who as president believed strongly enough in the limits of governmental and constitutional power, and particularly of federal power, to strenuously resist extending such authority—even when *he* would be the man to exercise it.

Coolidge believed that the property of a nation belonged to the citizens of that nation—and not to its government. He believed in strict obedience to the law, in service to others, in idealism rather than materialism.

Even in his own day, many dismissed Coolidge's notions of limited government as hopelessly outdated and unsophisticated. He didn't care. He meant what he said and said what he thought—and remains among the most pithily eloquent advocates for properly restrained government and taxation and concurrently for individual economic responsibility. He advocated a rigorously circumscribed federal government that empowered the American people to be free to be . . . free to be . . . well, free to be . . . whatever they *wanted* to be.

A simple philosophy.

So simple that it took humanity until the late eighteenth century to figure it out. So simple it only required the combined energies of a Washington, an Adams, a Jefferson, a Madison, a Hamilton, a Franklin— and a pretty good supporting cast behind them—to make it all work. So simple, that we seem to have forgotten it all. But as we glance back on what Mr. Coolidge articulated about such matters, we realize that not only could he clearly see what the Founders had devised, he could discern the broader human condition—and he could see ahead into the future, into a world where old verities, his verities, would quickly be discarded and disdained.

And he expressed what he discerned in fewer words, better chosen words, than just about anyone before or since.

Let's take one example—and a not particularly well-known one at that.

In January 1914, on being elected president of the Massachusetts Senate he informed his fellow legislators: "The normal must care for themselves."

The normal must care for themselves. Ah, what is he saying? That if you are a reasonable human you should be able to clothe and shelter and feed yourself. To make decisions for yourselves, about your future, about your children's future, about what you can do with your own money, about risks and choices. Adults *can* take care of themselves.

But note the subtext in the sentence: what about those who are not "normal?" They need help. They cannot adequately fend for themselves. And others—here is that concept of service again—must assist them. Preferably privately. Or, if that is not possible, only then through the auspices of government.

All of that in six words.

And he meant what he said. As Massachusetts lieutenant governor he dared to remark regarding the state's mental institutions: "Our party will have no part in a scheme of economy which adds to the misery of the wards of the commonwealth—the sick, the insane and the unfortunate—those who are too weak even to protest. Because I know these conditions I know a Republican administration would face an increasing state tax rather than not see them remedied."

But, of course, Calvin Coolidge never did raise taxes. Nor did he abandon or neglect the helpless wards of his commonwealth. Just the opposite happened. He *lowered* taxes again and again while providing needed services. He did this by practicing what he called "economy," a stringent attack on government waste and a refusal to fund programs that he found to be mere raids on the public treasury.

Yes, Coolidge was no "soak-the-rich" politician. "The method of raising revenue ought not to impede the transaction of business;" he said in his inaugural address, "it ought to encourage it. I am opposed to extremely high rates, because they produce little or no revenue, because they are bad for the country, and, finally, because they are wrong."

Again, he backed words with actions. American participation in World War I had skyrocketed the highest marginal tax rate from 7 percent to 77 percent. Coolidge's predecessor Warren Harding and Harding's (and later Coolidge's) Treasury Secretary Andrew Mellon cut that first to 56 percent and later 50 percent. Coolidge slashed it to 20 percent.

The results actually *aided* those of modest incomes. In 1920, the last year of Woodrow Wilson's administration, 15.4 percent of all personal income taxes were paid by those earning $5,000 a year or less. When Coolidge left office in 1929, that figure had shrunk to a miniscule 0.4 percent. Those earning $100,000 or more had paid 29.9 percent in 1920. By 1929 the figure had climbed to 65.2 percent. Ninety-eight percent of Americans now paid no income taxes at all. The burden of that tax had been shifted from the poor to the rich.

Calvin Coolidge cut taxes four times *and* produced a budget surplus each year of his presidency. He could do all this because he not only understood economics and government—he understood human nature. In February 1924, he told the National Republican Club:

> If we had a tax whereby on the first working day the Government took 5 per cent of your wages, on the second day 10 per cent, on the third day 20 per cent, on the fourth day 30 per cent, on the fifth day 50 per cent, and on the sixth day 60 per cent, how many of you would continue to work on the last two days of the week? It is the same with capital. Surplus income will go into tax-exempt

securities. It will refuse to take the risk incidental to embarking in business. This will raise the rate which established business will have to pay for new capital, and result in a marked increase in the cost of living. If new capital will not flow into competing enterprise, the present concerns tend toward monopoly, increasing again the prices which the people must pay.

He said more in that speech—so much more than a half century later economist Jude Wanniski would label it, "The most lucid articulation of the [supply-side] wedge model in modern times."

Ronald Reagan thought so much of Coolidge that he replaced a portrait of Harry Truman that had hung in the Cabinet Room with one of Silent Cal. "I . . . believe," Reagan wrote, "he has been badly treated by history. I've done considerable reading and researching of his presidency. He served this country very well and accomplished much . . ."

"He wrote simply, innocently, artlessly," H. L. Mencken once noted regarding Coolidge, "He forgot all the literary affectations and set down his ideas exactly as they came into his head. The result was a bald, but strangely appealing piece of writing—a composition of almost Lincolnian austerity and beauty. The true Vermonter was in every line of it."

And yet this master of articulation and plain-speaking has fallen victim to one of the most egregious misunderstandings of modern times, derided as a slavish worshiper of commercial interests.

"The chief business of the American people is business," Coolidge informed the American Society of Newspaper editors in January 1925, and for decades those words have been hung around his neck to "prove" his ultimate philistinism.

The words were wrenched out of context by historians with an axe to grind, and have been repeated by ignorant, sloppy, naïve, or lazy writers ever since.

Indeed, Coolidge did say "The chief business of the American people is business," but he was only warming up to his main point—a message at considerable variance from what he has been charged with saying and meaning.

Here is what Calvin Coolidge also said:

So long as wealth is made the means and not the end, we need not greatly fear it. And there never was a time when wealth was so generally regarded as a means, or so little regarded as an end, as today.

It is only those who do not understand our people who believe that our national life is entirely absorbed by material motives. We make no concealment of the fact that we want wealth, but there are many other things that we want very much more. We want peace and honor, and that charity which is so strong an element of all civilization. The chief ideal of the American people is idealism. I cannot repeat too often that America is a nation of idealists. . . . . No newspaper can be a success which fails to appeal to that element of our national life.

Idealism. Again, no mere word to Calvin Coolidge. Indeed, regarding a man who chose his words so carefully it is easy to believe there were *no* mere words. His entire adult life had been spent in public office—councilman, city solicitor, mayor, state representative, state senator, lieutenant governor, governor, vice-president, president—more offices than any other president ever held.

Yet, he sought office not to enrich himself or his ego but to serve. Until he occupied the White House, he lived in a rented half of a two-family house. It was not grand, but living grand was not what Calvin Coolidge was about.

"To him," wrote William Allen White, a not uncritical observer, "politics is what the sea is to the sailor, the woods to the forester, the family to the mother, an instinctive passion for some kind of service. [He] never has been turned into the accumulation of material things [instead observing] some inner monastic vow against owning much property."

"Coolidge rose to power," White noted, "not for Calvin Coolidge, the most powerful Republican in Massachusetts, the lawyer of Northampton, not for the father of the Coolidge children that they might have a better home, not for any material gain for Calvin Coolidge the man."

He used it for the public good.

But it was not easy for him to be a public man. To speak. To meet persons. To shake hands. To do what ordinary politicians do as a matter of course. A horrible shyness possessed Calvin Coolidge, possessed him from his earliest days, and never left him.

He never denied it. He told friends:

When I was a little fellow, as long as I can remember, I would go into a panic if I heard strange voices in the house. I felt I just couldn't meet people, and shake hands with them. Most of the visitors would sit with Mother and Father in the kitchen, and it was the hardest thing in the world to have to go through the kitchen door and give them a greeting. I was almost ten before I realized I couldn't go on that way. And by fighting hard I used to manage to get through that door. I'm all right with old friends, but every time I meet a stranger, I've got to go through the old kitchen door, back home, and it's not easy.

Yet he achieved more public offices—and won more elections—than any other president. And in doing so, he accomplished what he wanted, in the way he wanted to. He served without being servile.

Said the normally acerbic H. L. Mencken regarding Calvin Coolidge: "He begins to seem, in retrospect, an extremely comfortable and even praiseworthy citizen. His failings are forgotten; the country remembers only the grateful fact that he let it alone. Well, there are worse epitaphs for a statesman. If the day ever comes when Jefferson's warnings are heeded at last, and we reduce government to its simplest terms, it may very well happen that Cal's bones now resting inconspicuously in the Vermont granite will come to be revered as those of a man who really did the nation some service."

Amen.

REPUBLICAN STANDARD BEARERS
1924

FOR PRESIDENT.   FOR VICE-PRESIDENT.

— TWO GREAT AMERICANS —

Calvin Coolidge: A Biographical Portrait

Calvin Coolidge was born on the Fourth of July, July 4, 1872, in the miniscule, central Vermont hamlet of Plymouth Notch, a collection of perhaps a dozen dwellings, halfway between Ludlow and Bridgewater Corners. In other words, not particularly near anything, save maple syrup and hillsides.

He was not born poor nor rich, though by the standards of 1872 Plymouth Notch, his father, Colonel John Coolidge was a man of means, a general storekeeper, insurance agent, farmer, and politician, an individual of some local reputation.

Of his father Calvin would write:

My father had qualities that were greater than any I possess. He was a man of untiring industry and great tenacity of purpose. . . . He always stuck to the truth. It always seemed possible for him to form an unerring judgment of men and things. He would be classed as decidedly a man of character. I have no doubt he is representative of a great mass of Americans who are known only to their neighbors; nevertheless, they are really great. It would be difficult to say that he had a happy life. He never seemed to be seeking happiness. He was a firm believer in hard work. Death visited the family often, but I have no doubt he took a satisfaction in accomplishment and always stood ready to meet any duty that came to him. He did not fear the end of life, but looked forward to it as a reunion with all he had loved and lost.

Of his boyhood, Coolidge harbored no resentment, no sense that he might better have been born in another, more advantageous time or place. Regarding his rural neighbors, he wrote:

They drew no class distinctions except towards those who assumed superior airs. Those they held in contempt. . . .

It was all a fine atmosphere in which to raise a boy. As I look back on it[,] I constantly think how clean it was. There was little about it that was artificial. It was all close to nature and in accordance with the ways of nature. The streams ran clear. The roads, the woods, the fields, the people—all were clean. Even when I try to divest it of the halo which I know always surrounds the past, I am unable to create any other impression than that it was fresh and clean.

Tragedy, however, soon visited young Calvin's life. His mother, Victoria Josephine Moor Coolidge, a woman often in poor health, died in March 1885. He wrote:

It was her thirty-ninth birthday. I was twelve years old. We laid her away in the blustering snows of March. The greatest grief that can come to a boy came to me. Life was never to seem the same again.

In March 1890, Calvin's younger sister, Abigail also expired following a brief illness. The cause of her death most likely being appendicitis. She was fourteen.

Their deaths moved Calvin profoundly, forging a greater bond between surviving son and father, and, no doubt, reinforcing Calvin's already powerful, almost crippling, sense of shyness.

Educational opportunities at Plymouth Notch were limited to the cramped stone, one-room schoolhouse situated just up the road. "Few, if any, of my teachers reached the standard now required by all public schools," he would note, "They qualified by examination before the town superintendent. I first took this examination and passed it at the age of thirteen and my sister Abbie passed it and taught a term of school in a neighboring town when she was twelve years old."

Colonel Coolidge sent his son off to school to the modest Black River Academy, a few miles to the south in Ludlow and then much farther to the north, to the St. Johnsbury Academy in the state's Northeast Kingdom, and finally to college at Amherst, Massachusetts, where Coolidge's withdrawn Vermont ways proved both a puzzlement and an amusement to his more sophisticated and garrulous classmates.

His habits then were the habits of his future life, none of them particularly pointing the way toward a political, or any sort of public, career. A 1920 account of his life described the Amherst Coolidge thusly:

> Mindful always of the family self-denial, his college career was marked with persistent conscientiousness. He paid three dollars a week for his board, but only because he could not find a cheaper eating house.
>
> He was a quiet, unassuming man, unknown to many men during his first two years, but gradually winning the respect of the whole college.
>
> He was a keen student of the men about him whether they were professors, fellow students, or the people of the town. He had a fine sense of humor which he rarely used. He was a great reader of books, especially on history and government. His diligence in study precluded him from taking much of any part in the activities of the college outside of the regular work. Only in a modest way and as his leisure would permit did he enter into the so-called college life. He took no active part in sports.

He grew on his classmates, nonetheless, as he invariably grew on just about everybody, becoming known as a humorous and accomplished, if more than somewhat laconic, speaker. He graduated cum laude.

He endeavored to practice law but did not attend law school, instead clerking at law offices in Northampton, Massachusetts, a town a few miles south of Amherst. On passing the bar, he opened his own modest practice.

He entered politics, joining the local Republican committee, becoming city solicitor, and winning his first election—to the Northampton City Council, from Ward Two. "At least 400 Democrats voted for me," Calvin would write to his father. "Their leaders can't see why they did it. I know why. They knew I had done things for them, bless their honest Irish hearts." Later he accepted an appointment as Clerk of the Hampshire County Courts. Soon afterward, he became city Republican chairman.

Calvin Coolidge also took a wife. Grace Goodhue was nothing like Calvin, save for also hailing from Vermont—Burlington, to be exact —and, by fate, drifting also to Northampton. Outgoing and vivacious, educated at the University of Vermont, she taught at Northampton's Clark School for the Deaf. "I remember Grace Goodhue vividly . . ." recalled one

Northampton associate, the author Alfred Pearce Dennis, "[a] creature of spirit, fire, and dew, given to blithe spontaneous laughter, with eager birdlike movements, as natural and unaffected as sunlight or the sea, a soul that renders the common air sweet."

One day Grace Goodhue happened to be walking past Coolidge's bachelor lodgings, looked up, and saw him shaving—while wearing his derby hat. She laughed. He heard her. He saw her—and resolved to meet her.

He did, and—to the amazement of their friends—they courted. Alfred Pearce Dennis marveled:

> What did she see in him?—everybody asked. Certainly no Prince Charming or knight in shining armor. She saw, let us believe, as by swift divination that unseen thing which we call, for want of a better name, character. As by revelation, she apprehended what had to be beaten into the heads of the rest of us.

They married in her parents' parlor on October 4, 1905.

The newlyweds eventually engaged $27-per-month lodgings at 21 Massasoit Street, Northampton—half of a pleasant, but modest, white frame duplex:

> The days passed quietly with us until the next autumn [1906], when we moved into the house in Massasoit Street that was to be our home for so long. I attended to the furnishing of it myself, and when it was ready Mrs. Coolidge and I walked over to it. In about two weeks our first boy came on the evening of September seventh. The fragrance of the clematis which covered the bay window filled the room like a benediction, where the mother lay with her baby. We called him John in honor of my father. It was all very wonderful to us.

> We liked the house where our children came to us and the neighbors who were so kind. When we could have had a more pretentious home we still clung to it. So long as I lived there, I could be independent and serve the public without ever thinking that I could not maintain my position if I lost my office.

Their marriage produced another son, Calvin Jr., in 1908. John was the more reserved of their two offspring, the more like his father; Calvin Jr. the more outgoing.

All the while, Coolidge kept rising in politics. He won a term in the Massachusetts House. Taking his new legislative seat, he carried with him a letter of introduction, reading. "Like a singed cat he is better than he looks."

His political philosophy now began taking shape, as did his lifelong predilection to act without regard to political consequences. Of those days he recalled:

> When I first went to the Legislature I was a very young man. I suppose those who voted for me considered me a Radical or a Liberal. I had only been a member of the Legislature a few months when I made up my mind that Massachusetts at any rate was legislating faster than it could administer and that the sane thing was to call halt for the time being. I had not changed my views on these questions, but I had entirely changed my views as to what it was wise to do at the minute, and I changed my position and was probably called a conservative. I remember thinking at the time that neither the so-called liberals nor the so-called conservatives would understand me. Perhaps both would think I was dishonest or at least not firm in my convictions, and my career would end with that session of the Legislature. . . . Apparently they had more faith in me than I thought they would have.

When Northampton Republicans could find no other candidate for mayor, he won an upset victory to City Hall, where he cut taxes and raised teachers' salaries. From there it was back to Boston and a seat in the state senate. Within two years, he was elected senate president, not only with Republican votes, but also with substantial Democratic support. Said one Massachusetts labor leader regarding Coolidge, "In all my years of work in the Legislature I have never met a man [in] whose sense of justice and courage I had more trust."

While in the senate, Coolidge made a contact that would significantly impact his political career: Boston department store magnate Frank Waterman "Lord Lingerie" Stearns. Stearns, like Coolidge was an Amherst man. On first meeting Coolidge, Stearns found his manner off putting, but he soon came to regard Calvin as efficient, honest, a man of destiny, indeed, almost a second Lincoln.

By 1915, Coolidge, his eye on the governorship, was elected lieutenant governor. Three years later, he narrowly won the governorship and found himself confronted with two crises. The first involved a constitutional mandate to consolidate 118 government agencies into not more than twenty within three years—a political landmine. Coolidge not only avoided tripping any mines, he won accolades—and did it all within a single year.

The second and greater crisis involved Boston's restive police force. Chronically underpaid (Coolidge publicly admitted that "I do not approve of any strike. But can you blame the police for feeling as they do when they get less than a street car conductor?"), in violation of state law, police officers organized into a union. When, in September 1919, Boston Police Commissioner Edwin U. Curtis disciplined union leaders, police voted 1,134-to-2 to strike and 1,177 of the city's 1,544 police walked off the job, leaving the city unprotected. Violence and lawlessness followed. Boston Mayor Andrew J. Peters illegally removed Curtis from office (the police commissioner's appointment was a gubernatorial not a mayoral prerogative). Coolidge reinstated Curtis and called out the full State Guard, issuing these orders:

> The entire State Guard of Massachusetts has been called out. Under the Constitution, the Governor is Commander-in-Chief thereof, by an authority of which he could not, if he chose, divest himself. That command I must and will exercise. Under the law I hereby call on all the police of Boston who have loyally and in a never-to-be-forgotten way remained on duty to aid me in the performance of my duty of the restoration and maintenance of order in the City of Boston, and each of such officers is required to act in obedience to such orders as I may hereafter issue or cause to be issued. I call on every citizen to aid me in the maintenance of law and order.

Coolidge's actions broke the strike.

When American Federation of Labor President Samuel Gompers telegraphed Coolidge, demanding that the strikers be allowed to return to the positions they had abandoned, Coolidge responded:

BOSTON, MASS., Sept. 14, 1919

MR. SAMUEL GOMPERS

President American Federation of Labor, New York City, N.Y.

Replying to your telegram, I have already refused to remove the Police Commissioner of Boston. I did not appoint him. He can assume no position which the courts would uphold except what the people have by the authority of their law vested in him. He speaks only with their voice.

The right of the police of Boston to affiliate has always been questioned, never granted, is now prohibited. The suggestion of President Wilson to Washington does not apply to Boston. There the police have remained on duty. Here the Policemen's Union left their duty, an action which President Wilson characterized as a crime against civilization. Your assertion that the Commissioner was wrong cannot justify the wrong of leaving the city unguarded. That furnished the opportunity, the criminal element furnished the action. There is no right to strike against the public safety by anybody, anywhere, any time. You ask that the public safety again be placed in the hands of these same policemen while they continue in disobedience to the laws of Massachusetts and in their refusal to obey the orders of the Police Department. Nineteen men have been tried and removed. Others having abandoned their duty, their places have, under the law, been declared vacant on the opinion of the Attorney-General. I can suggest no authority outside the courts to take further action. I wish to join and assist in taking a broad view of every situation. A grave responsibility rests on all of us. You can depend on me to support you in every legal action and sound policy. I am equally determined to defend the sovereignty of Massachusetts and to maintain the authority and jurisdiction over her public officers where it has been placed by the Constitution and law of her people.

CALVIN COOLIDGE
Governor of Massachusetts

Coolidge's advisors thought his actions would alienate labor support and cost him re-election. He thought so too. He didn't care. "It does not matter whether I am elected or not," he replied matter-of-factly.

Instead, Coolidge's response—one sentence of it, really, "There is no right to strike against the public safety by anybody, anywhere, any time"—caught the imagination of the American public, electrifying the nation, stamping him as its no-nonsense champion of post-war law-and order. He swamped his Democratic opponent that November, winning 62 percent of the vote. Even Democratic President Woodrow Wilson wired him: "I congratulate you upon your election as a victory for law and order. When that is the issue, all Americans must stand together."

Unlike Wilson, Coolidge defended *all* Americans. "It is true that the German high command still couple American and African soldiers together in intended derision," he noted when running for governor in August 1918, "What they say in scorn, let us say in praise. We have fought before for the rights of all men irrespective of color . . . It would be fitting recognition of their worth to send our American Negro [soldiers], when that time comes, to inform the Prussian military despotism on what terms their defeated armies are to be granted peace." This Coolidge dared to say, while Woodrow Wilson aggressively segregated federal offices.

Calvin Coolidge's November 1919 landslide gubernatorial re-election fueled Frank Stearns' once unlikely ambition: to make his friend Calvin Coolidge President of the United States of America.

Stearns organized a Coolidge-for-President boomlet, hiring staffers, renting offices, and distributing handsomely bound compendiums containing Coolidge's public statements. Coolidge, never one to grasp for public office, disavowed Stearns' efforts. "I am not a candidate for the presidency," Coolidge announced, "I am Governor of Massachusetts, and am content to do my only duty, the day's work as such."

Nonetheless, Stearns kept plugging, skillfully employing his non-candidate candidate's terse eloquence to best advantage. Prior to that year's Republican National Convention he circulated copies of a brief collection of Coolidge's speeches, entitled *Have Faith in Massachusetts,* and featuring Calvin's January 1914 address to the Massachusetts state senate, to delegates, potential delegates and various Republican kingmakers. At the convention itself, Stearns circulated yet another such collection, this one entitled *Law and Order*, featuring his January 1920 inaugural address. "It was," admitted the head of Massachusetts' delegation, "as neat and effective a piece of political publicity as I have ever seen."

Calvin Coolidge's name was placed in nomination at the 1920 Republican National Convention. He might have garnered more support had he enjoyed the support of Massachusetts' Henry Cabot Lodge, convention chairman and majority leader of the United States Senate. Coolidge's simple tastes had not grown on Boston Brahmin Lodge. "Nominate a man who lives in a two-family house!" Lodge exploded, "Never! Massachusetts is not for him!"

Ohio's dark horse candidate, United States Senator Warren Gamaliel Harding, captured the nomination on the tenth ballot, but when time came to nominate a vice-president, weary delegates rebelled against designating mildly-progressive Wisconsin Senator Irvine L. Lenroot as Harding's running mate.

Thinking that Oregon delegate Wallace McCammant merely wished to second Lenroot's nomination, Temporary Convention Chairman Frank Willis of Ohio recognized Judge McCammant. He responded with this simple address:

> Mr. Chairman, Ladies and Gentlemen of the Convention: When the Oregon delegation came here instructed by the people of our State to present to this Convention as its candidate for the office of Vice-President a distinguished son of Massachusetts [Lodge] he requested that we refrain from presenting his name.
> But there is another son of Massachusetts who has been much in the public eye in the last year, a man who is sterling in his Americanism and stands for all that the Republican party holds dear, and on behalf of the Oregon delegation I name for the exalted office of Vice-President Governor Calvin Coolidge of Massachusetts.

Remarkably, that was enough to stampede the convention. Delegates spontaneously and enthusiastically nominated Coolidge.

"There goes Harding!" they said in the convention press box.

"What do you mean?"

"Harding'll never serve his term out. He'll die and Coolidge will be President."

"Don't be silly. What makes you say a thing like that?"

"Wait, you'll see. Coolidge luck. He's shot with it."

Coolidge, however, having once served as a lieutenant governor, had little desire to relocate to Washington and repeat the experience as vice president. When he received the news by phone, he turned to Grace and twanged, "Nominated for Vice President!"

"You don't mean it!" she responded, thinking it to be one of his jests.

"Indeed I do."

"You are not going to accept it, are you?"

"I suppose I shall have to," he replied, and, indeed, party loyalist that he was, he could not refuse it.

Also knowing the realities of the position was its current occupant, Woodrow Wilson's two-term Vice President Thomas R. Marshall. On July 16 Marshall telegraphed Coolidge: "Please accept my sincere sympathy."

On Sunday, June 13, Coolidge had written his father from Boston:

> MY DEAR FATHER:—I did not call you last night because it is so hard to talk from here to Plymouth. I knew you would have the news about as soon as I did anyway.
>
> Governor [Percival W.] Clement [of Vermont] called me right away. I hope you will not be disappointed. The enthusiasm of the convention is said to have been tremendous for me. The leaders had planned to name someone else but the convention ran away from them when an Oregon man nominated me, many other states followed and when Penn. was reached it gave me a majority. The cheering was very great and spontaneous.
>
> Men who were there say the convention wanted me for President. That was prevented by some of the Federal office holders who were bent on having one of their own and controlled enough votes to accomplish it.
>
> I am sure Senator Harding is a good man, and [he is] an old friend of mine. I hope you will not mind.
>
> Your Son, CALVIN COOLIDGE

The Warren Harding-Calvin Coolidge ticket, nonetheless, functioned harmoniously enough, with Harding pledging (quite truthfully, actually) that Coolidge would be the first vice-president to attend cabinet meeting.

Nonetheless, Coolidge remained loath to take time out from his gubernatorial duties. "I don't like it," he fumed, when Republican strategists proposed sending him on a southern campaign swing. "I don't like to speak. It's all nonsense. I'd much better be at home doing my work."

Nonsense or not, in November 1920 Harding and Coolidge, assisted by a massive public revulsion to Woodrow Wilson's dysfunctional administration, demolished Democratic standard bearers James M. Cox and Franklin D. Roosevelt, with 60 percent of the popular vote and 404-127 in the Electoral College.

The results were particularly pleasing in Massachusetts, where the Harding-Coolidge won triumphed, 681,153 to 276,691. Boston went Republican for the first time in 24 years. Democrats carried only two towns in the entire commonwealth. In Vermont, their ticket carried 75.8 percent of the vote and waltzed through Plymouth Notch 158–15.

Coolidge, nonetheless, chafed under his new office's inactivity. "I soon found that the Senate had but one fixed rule, subject to exceptions of course," he would ruefully write, "which was to the effect that the Senate would do anything it wanted to do whenever it wanted to do it. When I had learned that, I did not waste much time with the other rules, because they were so seldom applied." Unable to prove himself through accomplishment, official Washington saw him only as a silent little, red-headed man who Warren Harding would probably dump from the ticket in 1924.

Nonetheless, Coolidge had not been wasting his time. As his early biographer Edward Elwell Whiting noted of his vice presidential tenure:

> Mr. Coolidge took his duties as Vice-President precisely as he had taken other duties. He did the day's work. He did not seek publicity. That he kept informed in all national matters may have escaped the attention of the newspapermen who chose to forget him, but it was well understood by those who knew him best. . . . No man in Washington public life during the period of his vice-presidency was better informed as to political events or concerning the personalities and motives of members of the Senate. Whether the Senators realized that their presiding officer was studying them each and individually may be doubted; his friends knew it to be so. He knew what each Senator would be

likely to say or do. This applied to both parties. Few men have had a more accurate understanding of the United States Senate . . .

The Coolidge luck eventually struck—and, when it did, it struck in spades. Warren Harding died in August 1923, and Calvin Coolidge, vacationing at Plymouth Notch was sworn-in by kerosene light at 1:00 am by his seventy-eight-year-old notary public father. "I was awakened," wrote Coolidge, "by my father coming up the stairs calling my name. I noticed that his voice trembled. As the only times I had ever observed that before were when death had visited our family, I knew that something of the gravest nature had occurred." The modest ceremony complete, he trudged through the black Vermont night to visit his mother's grave. "I thought," he would recall, "I could swing it."

"The reporters withdrew," noted William Allen White, "the Coolidge house was darkened save for a light in the living room, and the Coolidges tried to sleep for a few hours until dawn. The President would not let the reporters photograph the inauguration. His taste always was good; his instincts decent and fine. After breakfast the reporters missed him. Then one of them saw him coming back from the little graveyard where his mother and sister lay. He had taken it all to them-the glory and the honor and the dread that must have gripped his heart. Slowly and abashed, staring at the ground, he passed the reporters and walked on into his new life."

Silent Cal did indeed swing it. Again, many underestimated him, prophesying that he would be denied re-nomination—as every accidental president save for Theodore Roosevelt had been. As president, Coolidge skillfully cleaned up the residue of scandal he inherited from the Harding administration—in the Justice Department, the Veterans Administration, the Department of Interior—the entire Teapot Dome mass. He restored public faith in government and sewed up the 1924 nomination. That November, the nation opted to "Keep Cool with Coolidge." Silent Cal easily defeated Democrat John W. Davis and the Progressive Party's Robert La Follette, garnering 54 percent of the popular vote—15,725,016 to 8,386,503 to 4,831,706—in the three-man race, 382 electoral votes to 136 for Davis and 13 for La Follette. Coolidge swept to victory in every state outside the Democratic South (save for "Fighting Bob" La Follette's Wisconsin) and in every county in New England. He even carried normally Democratic New York City, the last Republican presidential candidate to do so.

"The United States was not looking for either heroism or romanticism," said his biographer Claude Feuss, "What it wanted was plain ordinary common sense. Calvin Coolidge had character—and in the long run character outlasts what is temporarily spectacular."

Coolidge's often-maligned administration provided a wide variety of constructive measures and witnessed unprecedented economic growth, the "Coolidge Prosperity." His fiscal policy boasted unprecedented, and still unequalled, accomplishment. To recap:

- Reducing the national debt from $22.3 billion in 1923 to $16.9 billion in 1929.
- Reducing federal expenditures of $5.1 billion in 1921 to $3.3 billion in 1929.
- Cutting taxes four out of his six years as president.
- Reducing the highest effective tax rate from 50 percent (1922) to 20 percent but increasing revenue from that tax bracket from $77 million to $230 million.
- Slashing the tax burden on incomes under $10,000 from $130 million in 1923 to under $20 million in 1929; by 1927, 98 percent of the population paid no income tax.

"It is only a tiny exaggeration," noted historian Thomas B. Silver, "to say that Coolidge and [Treasury Secretary Andrew] Mellon completely removed the burden of federal income taxation from the backs of poor and working people between the time Coolidge entered the presidency and the time he left."

Coolidge's policies helped trigger a widely-based economic boom:

- Unemployment averaged 3.3 percent from 1922 to 1929.
- The Gross National Product increased annually by 7 percent from 1924 to 1929.
- Per capita income grew 30 percent from 1922 to 1928.
- Real earnings for employed wage earners increased 22 percent from 1922 to 1928.
- Industrial production increased 70 percent from 1922 to 1928.
- The average workweek decreased 4 percent from 1922 to 1928.
- Automobile ownership expanded three fold in the decade.

"Consumer prices rose at just 0.4 percent," noted syndicated columnist Cal Thomas in 1996, "During his term, there was a remarkable 17.5 percent increase in the nation's wealth. Total education spending in the United States rose fourfold. In the 1920s, illiteracy fell nearly in half. This was a golden age, by any standard."

Historian Paul Johnson summed it up: "Under Harding and still more under Coolidge, the USA enjoyed a general prosperity that was historically unique in its experience or that of any other society."

Coolidge's foreign policy carefully mixed isolationism and internationalism in a formula not only not very different from either his fellow Republican presidents Harding and Hoover, but also not very different from Franklin Roosevelt's pre-1939 initiatives. While opposing American participation in the League of Nations and United States diplomatic recognition of the Soviet Union (here he differed with FDR), Coolidge favored U.S. participation in the World Court. He avoided the growing threat of war with Mexico and restored good relations with that nation. He withdrew U.S. troops from Nicaragua, and broke precedent by personally attending the International Conference of American States in Havana. Capping his foreign initiatives were the Five-Power Naval Treaty (1923), the Dawes Plan for German Reparations (1924), and the Kellogg-Briand Pact which outlawed war as an instrument of foreign policy (1928).

Other highlights of the Coolidge presidency included:

- Vetoing the Veterans Bonus Bill.
- The Immigration Act of 1924.
- Legislation making Indians United States citizens.
- Proposing increased funding for aviation.
- Proposing construction of the St. Lawrence Seaway.
- The Jones-White Act of 1928 for construction of merchant ships.
- The Federal Radio Act, creating Federal Radio Commission.
- Proposing an anti-lynching law and a federal "Department of Education and Relief."
- Releasing the remaining Sedition Act violators convicted during the Wilson administration.
- Designating $250 million to construct public buildings resulting in Washington D.C.'s Federal Triangle.
- Dedicating Mount Rushmore.
- Authorizing construction of Hoover Dam.
- Twice vetoing the McNary-Haugen Farm Bill.

As always Coolidge kept his counsel, never committing to anything before he needed to, never saying anything before he might need to. A

Harvard-trained State Department official noted that Coolidge "listens to what one has to say and makes no comment. But if the ideas expressed appeal to him he acts on them weeks or months later. They are always stored in his mind, to be used when the opportunity occurs."

It was a time of accomplishment, of prosperity, indeed, of domestic tranquility. Yet Coolidge could not enjoy his presidency. The Coolidge luck ran out in June 1924, when sixteen-year-old Calvin Jr., playing tennis on the White House courts, developed a blister on his right foot. Infection and pathogenic blood poisoning resulted. From the very beginning the infection was serious, and, from its very onset, Coolidge seemed to know it. Vice-presidential nominee Charles Dawes was a guest at the White House on the evening the infection was diagnosed. He would later write, "As I passed the door of Calvin [Jr.]'s room, I chanced to look in. He seemed to be in great distress. The President was bending over the bed. I think I have never witnessed such a look of agony and despair as was on the President's face."

In an age without antibiotics, Calvin Jr. died that July 7. "In his suffering he asked me to make him well. I could not," his father would write, "When he went, the power and glory of the presidency went with him. . . . The ways of Providence are often beyond our understanding. It seemed to me that the world had need of the work that it was probable he could do. I do not know why such a price was exacted for occupying the White House."

Compounding the grief resulting from Calvin Jr.'s loss was the March 1926 death of Colonel John Coolidge. Calvin's father had been fading for months. "It is a nice bright day for the new year, but rather cold," Calvin wrote to him that January, "I wish you were here where you could have every care and everything made easy for you, but I know you feel more content at home. . . . I suppose I am the most powerful man in the world, but great power does not mean much except great limitations."

To escape Washington's summer doldrums, the Coolidges usually fled to cooler climes—to Plymouth Notch or Swampscott, Massachusetts, the Adirondacks, or Superior, Wisconsin—for weeks on end. In 1927, they summered in the Black Hills, and Tuesday, August 2, 1927, exactly four years to the day after he had become president, found Calvin Coolidge at a Rapid City, South Dakota high school classroom, handing out tiny slips of paper to amazed newsmen. Each read: "I do not choose to run for President in 1928."

He made the announcement without consulting Grace.

The political world cynically theorized that Coolidge was angling for a draft. He wasn't. In March 1929, Calvin Coolidge retired to Northampton, handing over the country to former Secretary of Commerce Herbert Hoover. He wasn't crazy about his successor. "Well, they're going to elect that superman Hoover," he told Starling, "and he's going to have some trouble. He's going to have to spend money. But he won't spend enough. Then the Democrats will come in and spend money like water. But they won't know anything about money. Then they will want me to come back and save money for them. But I won't do it."

Coolidge dabbled at law, earned a very lucrative $3,000 per week authoring a syndicated newspaper column, "Calvin Coolidge Says," and composed his tersely eloquent and, occasionally even poetic, memoirs, *The Autobiography of Calvin Coolidge.*

In returning his dues form for membership in Washington's National Press Club, he filled out the space marked "Occupation" with the word "Retired." Under "Remarks," he wrote: "Glad of it."

Calvin Coolidge's world was now a different world. He had moved back to 21 Massasoit Street, only to discover that an ex-President cannot live in a two-family house upon an ordinary small-town street. Autos, crowded with curiosity seekers, rolled by in constant procession. Admirers trampled his small lawn, trespassed upon his tiny porch, peered through his windows. He and Grace paid $40,000 to move to larger quarters, The Beeches, sixteen rooms on nine acres, overlooking the Connecticut River, a house far grander than Massasoit Street, far less grand than Pennsylvania Avenue.

It was there that he died in the early afternoon of January 5, 1933. Disturbed by the Great Depression, still saddened by his young son's passing, and possessing increasingly fewer reserves of energy, he returned home from his offices at noon. As he shaved, a heart attack felled him.

They buried Calvin Coolidge at Plymouth Notch, in the family graveyard, next to his mother and father and sister and youngest son, in the most humble grave of any United States President. No signs directed visitors. No gate around it. No words indicated the many offices he had held.

No words.

That is the way Calvin Coolidge would have wanted it.

"You Lose:"
The Coolidge Wit in Action

Alice Roosevelt Longworth, TR's rather acerbic daughter, once observed that Calvin Coolidge looked like he was "weaned on a sour pickle." In truth, he actually did, but often it was Silent Cal who had the last laugh on his critics. From grade school on, the dour, parsimonious Coolidge was underestimated by his rivals. Yet, slowly, imperceptibly, he rose from one public office to another until he reached the White House.

He ascended through hard work and through an unflinching integrity—but he was also assisted by a sharp, quick, and very dry wit. Will Rogers once observed that "Mr. Coolidge had more subtle humor than almost any public man I ever met. I have often said I would like to have hidden in his desk somewhere and just heard the sly little 'digs' that he pulled on various people that never got 'em at all. I bet he wasted more humor on folks than most anybody."

Rogers himself was once a victim of Cal's mordant wit. Will had invited the Coolidges to attend one of his shows, explaining that the evening basically consisted of him talking for a few hours, but also noting that he had a "fine quartet" to back him up.

"Yes," Coolidge deadpanned, "I like singing."

Here is a collection of stories involving the Coolidge wit—and just occasionally the wit of others concerning Silent Cal:

Once at a dinner party Coolidge was seated next to young woman who confided that she had bet that she could pry at least three words of conversation from him. Unimpressed, he quietly responded, "You lose."

***

Coolidge's skepticism regarding impassioned calls for more military spending paralleled his general frugality. At a Cabinet meeting he asked: "Why can't we just buy one airplane and have all the pilots take turns?"

Massachusetts Governor Channing Cox visited the White House, remarking to Coolidge how well organized he seemed to be.

"With all the people you have to see . . . " Cox noted, "and all the communications you have, you don't seem to be pressed for time at all. Now, back home in Massachusetts, I'm trying to fight all the time to get ahead, and get through, so I can do some *real* work."

"Channing," Coolidge replied, "the trouble is you talk back to them."

***

Coolidge provided similar advice to Herbert Hoover just after the 1928 Presidential election: "You have to stand every day three or four hours of visitors. Nine-tenths of them want something they ought not to have. If you keep dead-still they will run down in three or four minutes. If you even cough or smile they will start up all over again."

***

Speaking of advice and Hoover, Coolidge once remarked: "That man has given me nothing but advice and all of it bad."

***

When Coolidge became president upon the death of Warren Harding, his son Calvin Jr. was at work at a summer job in the tobacco fields surrounding Northampton, Massachusetts. One of the boy's co-workers demanded to know why. "If my father was President, I wouldn't be working in a tobacco field," he told young Calvin.

"You would if your father were my father," Coolidge Jr. responded.

***

Having served as Massachusetts lieutenant governor, Coolidge had a pretty clear perspective on what becoming Vice President meant. "I don't feel half as important," he noted, "as I did on the day I graduated from Black River Academy."

Senator Joseph Freylinghuysen of New Jersey desired to give Coolidge a gift. "I had some Havana cigars especially made for you in Cuba," he informed the President, "but there has been a delay in getting the lithographed bands with C.C. to go around them."

"Well, Joe," Coolidge responded, "you know I don't smoke the bands."

***

Former Navy Secretary Curtis Wilbur visited the White House and noticed Coolidge had installed a new rug, one with an elephant planted squarely in the middle of the design.

"Mr. President, what will be done with this rug if they elect a Democrat?" Wilbur wanted to know.

"Don't elect Democrats." Coolidge drawled back.

***

A good portion of Coolidge's duties as Vice President involved ceremonial matters, including substituting for President Harding at dinners Harding was too busy to attend. Someone asked Coolidge how he felt about dining out so often. "Got to eat somewhere," he responded.

***

In 1924 a contingent of show business folks came to the White House to endorse Calvin's election. Ethel Barrymore wanted to know what sort of president Coolidge thought he would make.

"I think the American people want a solemn ass as a president," Coolidge replied, "And I think I'll go along with them."

***

Shortly after Coolidge became President a messenger brought him his first paycheck for that office. Coolidge eyed it seriously, folded it in half, and carefully stuffed it in his pocket.

He looked up at the messenger, deadpanning, "Call again."

***

Job seekers had to be careful in approaching Coolidge. Once, a White House visitor asked Cal if he was familiar with a certain someone.

"A very interesting situation there," Cal noted, "He wants to go to London as ambassador. He spent half an hour telling me considerations that should win the appointment."

"I'm sure you were aware of the many considerations in his favor before," came the response.

"Yes," Coolidge twanged, "Less now."

***

When Coolidge attended Ludlow, Vermont's Black River Academy the institution featured the usual amount of schoolboy pranks, including the time a local cow found its way to the Academy's third floor. "I was never convicted of any of them," Coolidge said of these pranks, "and so must be presumed innocent."

***

Coolidge had a long memory. In 1904 the city of Northampton celebrated its two-hundredth and fiftieth anniversary. Governor John L. Bates visited City Hall for the occasion, and Calvin and Grace, then his fiancée, attended a reception provided in Bates' honor by the Daughters of the American Revolution. At one point, the couple ensconced themselves in what Coolidge considered "two comfortable vacant chairs." "A charming lady" then informed them that the chairs were reserved for Governor and Mrs. Bates.

Fourteen years later when Calvin was informed that he had won election to the governorship he turned to Grace and said, "The Daughters of the American Revolution cannot put us out of the Governor's chair now."

***

The most famous portrait of Grace Coolidge is that painted by Howard Chandler Christy, featuring not just the First Lady but also her handsome collie, Rob Roy. When Mrs. Coolidge donned a red dress so she might contrast with the pure white Rob Roy, the President impishly suggested that she wear a white dress and dye the dog red.

Despite the fact that the dog was not dyed crimson, Coolidge enjoyed the portrait so much that he had photographs made of it and sent to friends—including a copy to the man who had given him the animal. The man wired back: "Fine picture of dog. Send more photographs."

***

Illinois Congresswoman Ruth Hanna McCormick had been lobbying Coolidge to appoint a Chicagoan of Polish decent to a federal judgeship. To further pressure the President, she brought a group of Polish-Americans to the White House. The meeting didn't go well. The Poles didn't know what to say, and Coolidge was Coolidge—keeping his own counsel and staring at the floor. Finally he spoke: "Mighty fine carpet there." His audience seemed relieved and nodded their assent. "New one," Coolidge spoke again, "Cost a lot of money." The group again smiled in agreement. Then Coolidge got to the point: "She wore out the old one trying to get you a judge." With that the interview ended.

***

One day a Senator pointed over to the White House and jokingly asked President Coolidge who lived there.

"Nobody," Coolidge responded, "They just come and go."

***

On meeting a Senator who had just returned from Minnesota, Coolidge made a rare attempt at small talk, inquiring about the weather in the Midwest. When the Senator asked how the weather had been in Washington in his absence, Coolidge responded: "Well, it's been hot here. I was sitting here the other night with a lady who fainted. Don't know whether it was the weather or the conversation."

***

Once Coolidge was approached by a lady of society who exclaimed, "I'm from Boston."

"Yes," Coolidge drawled in reply, "And you'll never get over it."

After leaving the White House, Coolidge was mentioned for the post of Amherst College president. He wasn't interested. "Easier to control Congress than a college faculty," he replied.

***

When in January 1933 poet Dorothy Parker was informed that the quiet Coolidge had died, the waspish Algonquin Circle wit quipped: "How could they tell?"

***

Throughout his career Coolidge was his own man. Nobody knew that better than his "advisor" Boston department store owner Frank Stearns. When Coolidge was presented with a copy of *The Intimate Papers of Colonel House*—Edward M. House, being Woodrow Wilson's key advisor—he turned to Stearns and pointedly remarked, "an unofficial advisor to a President is not a good thing."

"Did I ever try to advise you?" Stearns asked.

"No," Coolidge replied, "but I thought I had better tell you."

***

The only election Calvin Coolidge lost was in 1905, just after he married Grace Goodhue, a contest for Northampton School Board. Afterwards a voter informed him, "I voted for your opponent because he has children in school and you don't."

"Might give me time," Coolidge responded.

***

As Massachusetts lieutenant governor, Coolidge presided over the State Senate. A clearly enraged Senator appeared before the podium, complaining about a fellow legislator: "He just told me to go to hell!"

"I've looked up the rules," Cal drawled, "and you don't have to do it."

***

After leaving the presidency Coolidge wrote a syndicated newspaper column, "Calvin Coolidge Says," but as his lucrative one-year contract was expiring he decided not to continue. Henry Stoddard, former publisher of the *New York Evening Mail*, was aghast and demanded to know why.

"I'll tell you a story about reasons," Coolidge responded, "A Massachusetts Governor some years ago appointed a judge. He named a young lawyer. The latter called and expressed his gratitude. 'There's just one piece of advice I care to give you as to your course on the bench,' said the Governor. 'Give your decisions—they may be right; but don't give your reasons—they may be wrong.' And so, I'm not going to give you my reasons. I've decided to stop."

***

When Coolidge was governor of Massachusetts, a Republican newspaperman told him this story:

> "When I was a boy in Springfield, another youngster met me on the street one day and asked me whether I was a Republican or a Democrat. I said I didn't know and asked what difference it made. 'Well,' said the other boy, 'if you are a Democrat you can march in our torchlight parade and come up to my father's flag-raising and have some ice cream.' I replied, 'All right, I'm a Democrat.' So you see, I sold my first vote to the Democratic Party for a dish of ice cream."

"Well," replied Coolidge, "you got more than some of the Democrats get."

***

Both Coolidge and his political opponents made hay out of his Silent Cal reputation. In the 1924 election Coolidge defeated Democrat John W. Davis and Progressive Robert "Fighting Bob" La Follette. La Follette's friend, Wisconsin Governor John J. Blaine, refused to attend Coolidge's inaugural, but Fighting Bob's friends in the Wisconsin legislature, nonetheless, passed an ironic tribute to Coolidge's election—two minutes of silence.

***

Coolidge distrusted flattery. A gentleman once presented him with a hickory-handled tool, blithering on about the handle, comparing the wood's qualities to those of Coolidge himself. Coolidge said nothing, looked the handle over slowly, and then pronounced one word, "Ash."

***

During Coolidge's 1920 vice-presidential campaign, his family received a Belgian police dog, Judy the First. Initially the two Coolidge boys—John and Calvin—attempted to send the dog to their paternal grandfather up in Vermont, but Colonel Coolidge refused the honor—which seemed to be just as well since the Coolidges were just as pleased to have Judy the First remain with them. Just before the election Calvin reported on the pooch to his father: "Your dog is growing well. She has bitten the ice man, the milkman, and the grocerman. It is good to have some way to get even with them for the high prices they charge for everything." A week and a half later, Calvin updated his father on events: "I had a picture sent to you of your dog taken with Grace. You will see she is a good dog. She has not bitten anyone lately so the trades people still come to the house."

***

Coolidge was riding in his official limousine in Washington's Rock Creek Park, when he noticed Idaho's Senator William Borah, a Republican legislator known for his extreme independence, on horseback. "Must bother the Senator to be going the same way as the horse," observed Coolidge.

***

In 1932 Coolidge spoke at Madison Square Garden in favor of Herbert Hoover's re-election. Afterwards a woman came up to him and told him how thrilled she was by his address. "I enjoyed it so much that I stood up all the time," she gushed.

"So did I," Coolidge deadpanned.

***

After Coolidge won the Northampton mayoralty, a Democrat offered congratulations. "I'm glad you were elected," he told Cal, "but I didn't vote for you."

Coolidge wasn't impressed by the sentiment. "Well, somebody did," he shot back.

***

Coolidge was no sportsman, but while in the White House he took a keen interest in fly-fishing. He spent the summer of 1928 on Wisconsin's Brule River. One day he reported to reporters that it contained an estimated 45,000 fish. Then he added: "I haven't caught them all yet, but I've intimidated them."

***

Speaking of hobbies, Coolidge was once asked what was his. "Holding office," he answered.

***

Just after Coolidge's ascension to the Presidency, James Reynolds, former treasurer of the Republican National Committee approached Coolidge. Reynolds had just been named vice-president of a small Washington, D.C. bank and wanted Coolidge to become a depositor, noting that even if Coolidge deposited even a small amount it would prove a great honor for his institution.

Coolidge puffed on his cigar and maintained—even for him—a discreet silence.

Finally, he spoke. "Couldn't you make me an honorary depositor?" he asked.

***

Coolidge was once invited to lay a cornerstone, a task he did not enjoy. He dutifully turned a spadeful of earth, but said nothing. The master of ceremonies asked if he had any comments. Coolidge looked down at the ground he had just dug into and replied, "That's a fine fishworm."

***

The story goes that after attending church one Sunday, Coolidge was asked if he enjoyed the service. He grunted yes. "Did the preacher give a good sermon?" Another grunt. Then came the question, "What did the preacher preach about?"

"Sin," came the terse response.

"Calvin, what did the preacher say about sin?" the now exasperated friend asked.

"He was agin it."[*]

***

Grace Coolidge's mother was not impressed by her son-in-law. When Grace and Cal announced their engagement, Mrs. Goodhue attempted a delaying action, strongly suggesting that the marriage be delayed a year while Grace learned such domestic arts as the baking of bread.

"I believe they sell bread in stores," Calvin responded.

***

Grace Coolidge was convinced that her husband employed his sense of humor largely for her own amusement. "I know that is true," she once recalled, "of one characteristic comment which I heard him make, and it was uttered in so low a tone I almost missed it.

"Across the street from us lived a Smith College professor who had been a missionary in Palestine for nine years before he came to Smith. He had many interesting stories to tell of his experiences there. My mother was always a wonderful listener. One Sunday afternoon we were all sitting on the front porch when the professor came across the street to pay us a neighborly call. Finding an eager listener in Mother, he was soon launched upon one of his favorite topics. After a while, Mr. Coolidge quietly withdrew into the house. The neighbor talked on until twilight.

"After supper, when the family was seated around the evening lamp, Mother had much to say of Professor Grant and his talk about Palestine. From behind his paper I heard my husband mumble, 'He's used to talking to the heathen.'"

---

[*] This story, one of the more famous Coolidge anecdotes is apocryphal. "I happened to be present the first time the President heard it," Grace Coolidge once recalled, "He laughed mildly and remarked that it would be funnier if it were true." Unverified and, also quite likely apocryphal, is his alleged observation, "When a great many people are unable to find work, unemployment results."

***

After Grace and Cal married, Grace came up to Grace carried a goodly-sized leather bag. He tipped it over and out flowed a batch of socks that needed mending. Grace jokingly wanted to know if that was why he had married her. "No," he responded, "but I find it mighty handy."

***

Not surprisingly, Coolidge tried to inculcate the habit of thrift in his two sons. Walking past a Northampton bank where the boys had small savings accounts, Coolidge bade them stop. "Boys," he said, listen here a minute and maybe you can hear your money working for you."

***

Shortly after she gave birth to her first child, Grace bought a volume entitled *Our Family Physician* for the then exorbitant price of $8.00 but feared telling her husband of her extravagance. A few weeks later she opened the book and found written on the flyleaf: "Don't see any recipe here for curing suckers! Calvin Coolidge."

***

Grace Coolidge delegated much of the family cooking to her housekeeper. But in the ninth year of the Coolidge marriage, the housekeeper took ill, and Grace pitched in to make an apple pie—whose crust was by her own admission "a trifle tough." This did not escape her husband's notice. That night two of Grace's friends visited. Calvin solicitously inquired if they would care for any dessert. They said yes, and Coolidge led them into the dining room where he had neatly laid out pie, silverware, and napkins. Clearly, he was pulling out all the stops to rid the household of Grace's concoction. When his guests had finished, he asked, "Don't you think the road commissioner would be willing to pay my wife something for her recipe for piecrust?"

***

Cal and Grace settled gingerly into their life as President and First Lady following Warren Harding's death, but after a couple weeks something began to gnaw at Mrs. Coolidge: her husband wouldn't tell her what his daily schedule was. Neither would anyone else. "Calvin, I wish you would have your secret service men give me your engagements," she mildly commented.

"Grace," he husband responded, "we don't give that out promiscuously."

***

The grounds at 1600 Pennsylvania Avenue included some stables, and at one point in the Coolidges' White House tenure, Grace decided to take advantage of the situation.

The next day the front page of a local paper headlined, "Mrs. Coolidge Takes Up Riding."

"It had the semblance of a death notice," Grace would write, "It certainly resulted in tolling a death knell to my hopes, when the President, seated at the opposite side of the breakfast table, unfolded his paper and read at my latest venture.

"With a look of surprise mingled with anxiety and disapproval, he dashed my adventurous sprit with, 'I think you will find that you will get along at this job fully as well if you do not try anything new.'"

***

A Baptist minister dined at the Coolidges'—but merely picked at his food, contending abstinence aided his sermons. Coolidge went to hear him, reporting back: "Might as well have et."

***

Coolidge could be deeply sentimental, but he had no intention of showing it, even at anniversaries or Christmas. Grace recalled that the only time she received an anniversary present from her husband she was on her way to the theatre with Mrs. Frank Stearns. "I thought it was some sort of a joke," she recalled, "for the size and shape of the package indicated a toothbrush."

It turned out to be a gold and platinum bracelet.

***

One Christmas when Coolidge was President, he presented his wife with twenty-five one dollar gold coins. Accompanying the gift was a card with Frank Stearns name on it, reading, "Compliments of the Season."

"I thought that I recognized it as the card which had come with a box of neckties from Mr. Stearns for Mr. Coolidge a day or two before," Grace noted, "Later investigation proved I was right."

***

One evening Secret Service agent Edmund Starling noticed that Secretary of the Navy Edwin Denby was working late. The next day Starling remarked to Coolidge that Denby often stayed late, adding "He must be an excellent man for the job."

"I wouldn't say that," the President responded, "I don't work at night. If a man can't finish his job in the day he's not smart."

***

Coolidge liked Starling and would often make cheese sandwiches for him, using a particularly sharp cheese he had sent from Vermont. One day he said to the Secret Service man: "I'll bet no other President of the United States ever made cheese sandwiches for you."

"No," Starling responded, "It is a great honor."

Then, Coolidge added, "I have to furnish the cheese too."

***

In 1930 Coolidge toured California. In Los Angeles he received a letter waning him he would be assassinated. He calmly handed it to a nearby guard, saying, "Guess this belongs to you."

***

A well-known journalist had strenuously lobbied Coolidge for an exclusive interview. Cal finally granted the request, only to respond to each question with a terse "no comment." With the ordeal concluded, Coolidge bid farewell to his interrogator, saying "By the way, don't quote me."

When Coolidge visited the Black Hills, some locals presented him with a cowboy outfit. Coolidge decided to have his picture taken in it.

His aides were aghast.

"But I don't see why you object," Coolidge responded, "The people here have sent me this costume and they wouldn't have sent it unless they expected me to put it on. Why shouldn't I have my picture taken with it to please them?"

"It's making people laugh," came an exasperated reaction.

"Well, it's good for people to laugh."

(collection of the author)

Quotes from Silent Cal

Yes, Calvin Coolidge could be terse.

"You could sit with him on a three-hour train ride from Northampton to Boston and really enjoy his companionship although he never said a word," recalled one friend, "With most any other man you would have had the fidgets, the quietness would have become tense.

"But with him quietness was never assumed; it was as natural as breathing. And the queer part of it is that he was always seeking out companionship even though he did not want to talk. He always seemed to be a lonely man. If there were ten vacant seats in a railroad car, he would walk disconsolately down the aisle, seeking an acquaintance, sidle into the seat with him, and relapse into solemn silence." Yet while Calvin Coolidge wasn't exactly talkative nor was he the Silent Cal of modern mythology. When occasion demanded, Calvin Coolidge knew how to employ the English language to a spectacular extent.

Coolidge was the last president to write all his own speeches—and he delivered more of them than any of his predecessors. As president he held 520 press conferences—eight per month. His formal inauguration address was expected to set a record for brevity. Instead his 4,059 words edged Warren Harding's 3,318 words and the 3,328 words of Woodrow Wilson's *two* inaugurations. It is not entirely ironic that a collection of Coolidge's press conference transcripts is entitled *The Talkative President*.

Over the course of a three-decade long political career, he provided his opinion on any number of topics, never wasting nor mincing words.

Here is what Silent Cal had to say:

ADVANCEMENT

"One should never trouble about getting a better job. But one should do one's present job in such a manner as to qualify for a better job when it comes along."

Coolidge: An American Enigma p. 80

ADVERTISING

"Goods not worth advertising are not worth selling."

Calvin Coolidge Says December 6, 1930

AGRICULTURE

"No complicated scheme of relief, no plan for Government fixing of prices, no resort to the public Treasury will be of any permanent value in establishing agriculture."

Adequate Brevity p 12

ALASKA

"It is my information that one in every eleven of the white people that live in Alaska are on the Federal payroll. Business is not brisk up there. There are some fisheries there and some mining, but we are spending $11,000,000 a year so I think the best line of endeavor that there is in Alaska is to get on the Federal payroll. Now I presume it is unconscious, but a condition of that kind would stimulate an activity on the part of those that aren't on the payroll to criticism of those that are, in order that a change might be made to their advantage, so that whenever there are protests against Federal officers up there they have to be viewed with that in mind."

November 20, 1925—The Talkative President pp. 233-34

AMERICA

"America follows no such delusion as a place in the sun for the strong by the destruction of the weak. America seeks rather, by giving of her strength for the service of the weak, a place in eternity."

Autobiography of Calvin Coolidge p. 121

"America has been a success."

November 1, 1919—Have Faith in Massachusetts p. 268

"It is sometimes assumed that Americans care only for material things, that they are bent only on that kind of success which can be cashed into dollars and cents. That is a very narrow and unintelligent opinion. We have been successful beyond others in great commercial and industrial enterprises because we have been a people of vision. Our prosperity has resulted not by disregarding but by maintaining high ideals. Material resources do not, and cannot, stand alone; they are the product of spiritual resources. It is because America, as a nation, has held fast to the higher things of life, because it has had a faith in mankind which it has dared to put to the test of self-government, because it has believed greatly in honor and righteousness, that a great material prosperity has been added unto it."

July 6, 1922—The Price of Freedom p. 174

"There is no reason for Americans to lack confidence in themselves or their institutions. Let him who doubts them look about him. Let him consider the power of his country, its agriculture, its industry, its commerce, its development of the arts and sciences, its great cities, its enormous wealth, its organized society, and let him remember that all this is the accomplishment of but three centuries. Surely we must conclude that here is a people with a character which is not to be shaken."

July 6, 1922—The Price of Freedom p. 181

"America seeks no earthly empire built on blood and force. No ambition, no temptation, lures her to thought of foreign dominions. The legions which she sends forth are armed, not with the sword, but with the cross. The higher State to which she seeks the allegiance of all mankind is not of human, but of divine origin. She cherishes no purpose save to merit the favor of Almighty God."

Inaugural Address, March 4, 1925
Messages and Papers of the Presidents p. 9488

"There has been abroad many times some criticism of our Government, of our people, and our ways, but that has demonstrated, I think, that when they are in real trouble and real difficulty over there, they turn to us as a nation that will be fair with them—one in whose judgment and in whose character they can rely; and notwithstanding differences that have seemed to exist, they are willing to abide by the faith that they have in us, and I think it is a very substantial accomplishment."

December 11, 1923—The Talkative President p. 181

"We do not need to import any foreign economic ideas or any foreign government. We had better stick to the American brand of government, the American brand of equality, the American brand of wages. America had better stay American."

To labor leaders, September 1, 1924
The Mind of the President p. 190

"The encouraging feature of our country is not that it has reached our destination, but that it has overwhelmingly expressed its determination to proceed in the right direction."

Inaugural Address, March 4, 1925
Messages and Papers of the Presidents p. 9488

"In the fullness of time America was called into being under the most favorable circumstances, to work out the problem of a more perfect relationship among mankind, that government and society might be brought into harmony with reason and conscience."

Adequate Brevity p. 9

"Our first duty is to ourselves. American standards must be maintained. American institutions must be preserved."

Adequate Brevity p. 10

"The trial which the civilization of America is to meet does not lie in adversity. It lies in prosperity. It will not be in a lack of power, but in the directing the use of great power. There is new danger in our very greatness."

Adequate Brevity p. 45

"It is our desire to make America more American. There is no greater service that we can render the oppressed of the earth than to maintain inviolate the freedom of our citizens."

Adequate Brevity p. 58

"Our country, our people, our civil and religious institutions may not be perfect, but they are what we have made them. They are good enough so that it has been necessary to build a high exclusion law to prevent all the world from rushing in to possess them."

Calvin Coolidge Says June 30, 1930

"The higher of standards, the greater our progress, the more we can do for the world."

Calvin Coolidge Says July 23, 1930

AMERICANISM

"We have been, and propose to be, more and more American. We believe that we can best serve our own country and most successfully discharge our obligations to humanity by continuing to be openly and candidly, intensely and scrupulously, American."

Inaugural Address, March 4, 1925

AMERICAN REVOLUTION

"If the American Revolution meant anything, it meant the determination to live under a reign of law. It meant the assertion of the right of the people to adopt their own constitutions, and when so adopted, the duty of all the people to abide by them."

Adequate Brevity p. 11

"The meaning of the American Revolution is now clear to us; it was conservative; it had as its purpose the preservation of the ancient rights of English freemen, which were not new even when they were set out in the Great Charter of the day of King John; it represented an extension of the right of the people to govern themselves."

Adequate Brevity p. 11

AMERICANS

"There's too ready a hearing abroad for Americans who make a habit of criticizing their own country."

To newspaperman Herman Beaty, *Meet Calvin Coolidge* p. 177

ANCESTORS

" . . . we do not choose our ancestors."

Autobiography of Calvin Coolidge p. 37

APPEARANCE

"In public life it is sometimes necessary to appear really natural to be actually artificial."

Autobiography of Calvin Coolidge p. 20

ATHEISM

"It is hard to see how a great man can be an atheist. Without the sustaining influence of faith in a divine power we could have little faith in ourselves. We need to feel that behind us is intelligence and love. Doubters do not achieve; skeptics do not contribute; cynics do not create. Faith is the great motive power, and no man realizes his full possibilities unless he has the deep conviction that life is eternally important, and that his work, well done, is a part of an unending plan."

Foundations of the Republic p. 68

AUTHORITY

"Can those entrusted with the gravest authority set any example save that of the sternest obedience to the law?"

Adequate Brevity p. 15

"The authority of the law is questioned these days all too much. The binding obligation of obedience against personal desire is denied in many quarters. If these doctrines prevail all organized government, all liberty, all security are at an end."

Adequate Brevity p. 15

BANKS

"Every banker knows that to depend on the business and patronage of the rich would be vain, that if any success attends his efforts it must be by serving and doing the business of the people."

June 27, 1921—*The Price of Freedom* p. 51

BASEBALL

"We pitch with the pitchers, we go to bat with the batters and we make a home run with the hard hitters. The training, the energy, the intelligence which these men lavish upon their craft ought to be an inspiration in every walk of life. They are a great band, these armored knights of the bat and ball. They are held up to a high standard of honor on the field, which they have seldom betrayed.

"While baseball remains our national game, our national tastes will be on a higher level and our ideals on a firmer foundation."

Washington, D.C., October 11, 1924

"Baseball is our national game. It is peculiarly a local product with the widest popular appeal of any sport. This is because every play can be seen and the game is so easily comprehended that all its fine points can be appreciated. Moreover, while the expense of maintaining a professional team is very great, attendance is so large that admissions remain at popular prices.

"It is natural to enjoy a contest. But the interest is not only from the matching of the skill of the opposing teams. Although the spectators do not touch the ball they nevertheless play a prominent part. Even a championship match with only one beholder would not be baseball. The outdoor air and the relaxation from care are partly the attraction. We go to the game in the hope that with three men on base the batter for our team will drive the ball over the fence so that we can revel in the intoxication of crowd delirium. That is the common touch of nature reaching from the street urchin to the President which lures us all to the ball field.

"While the national sport flourishes we can be sure the race is not growing old."

Calvin Coolidge Says October 2, 1930

BIGOTRY

"Bigotry is only another word for slavery. It reduces to serfdom not only those against whom it is directed, but also those who seek to apply it. An enlarged freedom can only be secured by the application of the golden rule. No other utterance ever presented such a practical rule of life."

Third Annual Message to Congress, December 8, 1925
Messages and Papers of the Presidents p. 9537

BOLSHEVISM

"Profitable employment is the death blow to Bolshevism . . ."

October 4, 1919—*Have Faith in Massachusetts* p. 244
Adequate Brevity p. 17

"Not all those who are working to better the condition of the people are Bolsheviki or enemies of society."

October 4, 1919—*Have Faith in Massachusetts* p. 243

"The world has been greatly shaken in the past decade. [The forces of creation and redemption] have been tested as they never before were tested. The wonder is not that Russia, under a comparatively new organization which had never reached down to the heart of the people, collapsed; the wonder is that the world as a whole has stood firm . . ."

June 7, 1922—*The Price of Freedom* p. 167

BUDGET, BALANCED

"The people ought to take no selfish attitude of pressing for removing moderate and fair taxes which might produce a deficit. We must keep our budget balanced for each year. That is the cornerstone of our national credit, the trifling price we pay to command the lowest rate of interest of any great power in the world. Any surplus can be applied to debt reduction, and debt reduction is tax reduction."

Messages and Papers of the Presidents p. 9723

BUSINESS

"After all, the chief business of the American people is business. They are profoundly concerned with producing, buying, selling, investing, and prospering in the world. I am strongly of the opinion that the great majority of people will always find these are moving impulses in our life. . . . In all experience, the accumulation of wealth means the multiplication of schools, the encouragement of science, the increase of knowledge, the dissemination of intelligence, the broadening of outlook, the expansion of liberties, the widening of culture. Of course the accumulation of wealth cannot be justified as the chief end of existence. But we are compelled to recognize it as a means to well-nigh every desirable achievement. So long as wealth is made the means and not the end, we need not greatly fear it.

And there never was a time when wealth was so generally regarded as a means, or so little regarded as an end, as today.

"It is only those who do not understand our people who believe that our national life is entirely absorbed by material motives. We make no concealment of the fact that we want wealth, but there are many other things that we want very much more. We want peace and honor, and that charity which is so strong an element of all civilization. The chief ideal of the American people is idealism. I cannot repeat too often that America is a nation of idealists. . . . . No newspaper can be a success which fails to appeal to that element of our national life."

To the American Society of Newspaper Editors,
January 17, 1924, Washington, D.C.
Calvin Coolidge: Man From Vermont p. 358

"It would be contrary to sound policy for business for business or any organization to engage in an effort to dominate political or governmental action by meddling in what does not concern them. That would warrant a revival of criticism against invisible government. But when industry will be affected by governmental action it might be heard sympathetically and without implication of seeking domination contrary to public interest. We cannot have employment and prosperity except on the basis of justice to business."

Calvin Coolidge Says December 30, 1930

"The government has never shown much aptitude for real business. The Congress will not permit it to be conducted by a competent executive, but constantly intervenes. The most free, progressive and satisfactory method ever devised for the equitable distribution of property is to permit the people to care for themselves by conducting their own business. They have more wisdom than any government."

Calvin Coolidge Says January 5, 1931

BUSINESS, MINDING ONE'S

"Perhaps one of the most important accomplishments of my administration has been the minding of my own business."

March 1, 1929—*The Talkative President* p. 19

CAPITAL

"Invested capital is the result of brains."

Adequate Brevity p. 18

"Capital is the chief material minister to the general character of all mankind."

Adequate Brevity p. 18

CARNEGIE, ANDREW

"He offered opportunity. He knew it was all his beneficiaries could profitably receive. If they were to have life more abundantly he knew it could only come through their own effort. He could not give the means by which others could provide for themselves. He did not pauperize. He ennobled."

April 28, 1921—*The Price of Freedom* p. 43

CHANGE

"There is considerable speculation as to whether I am likely to change or not. I don't anticipate to change very much. I have tried in the conduct of my office to be natural and I don't want to change that attitude. There are two or three people that have served with me in the conduct of affairs of the United States that I should be pleased if they changed a little—that I have to change from saying 'no' to saying 'yes.'"

November 11, 1924—*The Talkative President* p. 11

CHARACTER

"There is no surer road to destruction than prosperity without character."

July 7, 1921—*The Price of Freedom* p. 64

"We must forever realize that material rewards are limited and in a sense they are only incidental, but the development of character is unlimited and is the only essential."

Adequate Brevity p. 18

"Character is the only secure foundation of the state."

Speech at a New York City Lincoln Day Dinner, February 12, 1924

"Honest poverty is one thing, but lack of industry and character is another."

Armistice Day Address, Kansas City, Missouri, November 11, 1926
Messages and Papers of the Presidents p. 9605

"That which we call character in all men, is not a matter of hire and salary."

Adequate Brevity p. 18

CHARITY

"The recognition of brotherhood brings in the requirement of charity. But it is only on the basis of individual property that there can be charity. Our very conception of the term means that we deny ourselves of what belongs to us, in order to give it to another. If that which we give is not really our own, but belongs to the person to whom we give it, such an act may rightfully be called justice, but it cannot be regarded as charity."

Foundations of the Republic p. 109

CHURCH MEMBERSHIP

"Although I had been rather constant in my attendance, I had never joined the church . . . . Among other things, I had some fear as to my ability to set that example which I always felt ought to denote the life of a church member. I am inclined to think now that this was the counsel of darkness."

Autobiography of Calvin Coolidge p. 179

CITIZENSHIP

"After all, good citizenship is neither intricate nor involved; it is simple and direct; it is every-day common sense and justice."

Adequate Brevity p. 19

CIVILIZATION

"The process of civilization consists of the discovery by men of the laws of the universe, and of living in harmony with these laws."

Adequate Brevity p. 20

"The law of progress and civilization is not the law of the jungle. It is not an earthly law, it is a divine law. It does not mean the survival of the fittest, it means the sacrifice of the fittest. Any mother will give her life for her child. Men put the women and children in the lifeboats before they themselves will leave the sinking ship."

Adequate Brevity p. 21

"Civilization is always on trial, testing out, not the power of material resources, but whether there be, in the heart of the people, that virtue and character which comes from charity sufficient to maintain progress."

Adequate Brevity p. 21

COMMERCE

"Where commerce has flourished there civilization has increased."

April 11, 1916—*Have Faith in Massachusetts* p. 16

"To-day it is not the battle fleet, but the mercantile fleet which in the end will determine the destiny of nations."

April 11, 1916—*Have Faith in Massachusetts* p. 17

COMMISSIONS

"When I talk with people that I appoint to commissions and tell them that I would like to have them go on to the various boards with the idea that they may be abolished, they say they ought to be abolished, but when they have taken their position they very soon change their mind."

August 9, 1927—*The Talkative President* p. 76

COMMUNISM

"Communism will fail because what it attempts is against human nature. No man will provide me with food and other necessities of life unless he is a gainer by it in some way."

To newspaperman Herman Beaty, *Meet Calvin Coolidge* p. 178

COMMUNISTS

"I have a question here as to whether communists ought to be allowed to come into this country if they come in for commercial purposes. Well, I rather think that that question would answer itself. The only thing that the Government is trying to do is to see that our laws are observed. It isn't trying to enforce its own ideas or carry out its own desires about people that can come in or stay out. The fact that a person was going to come here and spend a large sum of money I don't think would make any difference in the law. I don't know of any provision in the law that says the right to come into this country is for sale, that the principles of the United States are for sale if you want to pay enough and you don't have to live according to the laws of this country."

September 22, 1925—*The Talkative President* p. 259

CONSTITUTION

"The Constitution is the sole source and guaranty of national freedom."

Accepting the presidential nomination, Washington, August 4, 1924

"To live under the American Constitution is the greatest political privilege that was ever accorded to the human race."

At the White House, December 12, 1924

"Some people do not seem to understand fully the purpose of our constitutional restraints. They are not for protecting the majority, either in or out of the Congress. They can protect themselves with their votes. We have adopted a written constitution in order that the minority, even down to the most insignificant individual, might have their rights protected. So long as our Constitution remains in force, no majority, no matter how large, can deprive the individual of the right of life, liberty or property, or prohibit the free exercise of religion or the freedom of speech or of the press. If the authority now vested in the Supreme Court were transferred to the Congress, any majority no matter what their motive could vote away any of these most precious rights. Majorities are notoriously irresponsible. After irreparable damage had been done the only remedy that the people would have would be the privilege of trying to defeat such a majority at the next election. Every minority body that may be weak in resources or unpopular in the public estimation, also nearly every race and religious belief, would find themselves practically without protection, if the authority of the Supreme Court should be broken down and its powers lodged with the Congress."

Address dedicating a monument to Lafayette, September 6, 1924

CONVERSATION

"Many times I say only 'yes' or 'no' to people. Even that is too much. It winds them up for twenty minutes or more."

To Bernard Baruch, *Meet Calvin Coolidge* p. 133

COOLIDGE, GRACE

"For almost a quarter of a century she has borne with my infirmities, and I have rejoiced in her graces."

Autobiography of Calvin Coolidge p. 93

COOLIDGE, COL. JOHN

"My father had qualities that were greater than any I possess. He was a man of untiring industry and great tenacity of purpose . . . He always stuck to the truth. It always seemed possible for him to form an unerring judgment of men and things. He would be classed as decidedly a man of character. I have no doubt he is representative of a great mass of Americans who are known only to their neighbors; nevertheless, they are really great. It would be difficult to say that he had a happy life. He never seemed to be seeking happiness. He was a firm believer in hard work. Death visited the family often, but I have no doubt he took a satisfaction in accomplishment and always stood ready to meet any duty that came to him. He did not fear the end of life, but looked forward to it as a reunion with all he had loved and lost."

Your Son Calvin Coolidge p. vii

"The lines he laid out were true and straight, and the curves regular. The work he did endured."

Autobiography of Calvin Coolidge p. 12

COOLIDGE, JOHN (SON) (INSTRUCTIONS REGARDING COLLEGE)

"My dear John:—

Some weeks ago I wrote you a letter. You have made no response to it whatever. When I send you some instructions I want to know that you are carrying them out.

Now I want to know how much time you are spending in Northampton. I would like to know what entertainments you are attending and who you are taking them with you there and at Amherst.

I want you to keep in mind that you have been sent to college to work. Nothing else will do you any good. Nobody in my class who spent their time in other ways has ever amounted to anything. Unless you want to spend your time working you may just as well leave college. Nothing else will make you a man or gain for you the respect of people.

I want you to refuse all requests that will interfere with your doing the work that is assigned each day for you to do.

Your father

Calvin Coolidge"

To John Coolidge, October 12, 1924
Your Son Calvin Coolidge pp. viii-ix

COURTS

"Courts are established, not to determine the popularity of a cause, but to adjudicate and enforce rights."

January 7, 1914—Have Faith in Massachusetts p. 4

CRITICISM

"Destructive criticism is always easy because, despite some campaign oratory, some of us are not yet perfect."

April 11, 1916—*Have Faith in Massachusetts* p. 16

"I do not care to be criticizing those in power. I've never been much good attacking men in public office. If they succeed, the criticism fails; if they fail, the people find it out as quickly as you can tell them."

To Henry Stoddard, December 14, 1932, *Meet Calvin Coolidge* p. 214

"If we judge ourselves only by our aspirations and everyone else only their conduct we shall soon reach a very false conclusion. When we have exhausted the possibilities of criticism on ourselves it will be time enough to apply it on others."

Calvin Coolidge Says, July 18, 1930

CYNICISM

"There is no place for the cynic or the pessimist. Who is he that can take no part in business because he believes it selfish? Who is he that can take no part in religion because he believes it is imperfect? These institutions are the instruments by which an eternal purpose is working out the salvation of the world. It is not for us to regard them with disdain; it is for us to work with them. It is a high calling in which to be even a doorkeeper is better than to rule over many multitudes of critics and philistines."

June 7, 1922—*The Price of Freedom* p. 169

DANCING

"I approve of people that like to dance dancing as much as they wish."

December 23, 1924—*The Talkative President* p. 40

DEBT

"Debt reduction is tax reduction."

Fifth Annual Message to Congress, December 6, 1927
Messages and Papers of the Presidents p. 9723

DEFENSE

"America represents the greatest treasure that there is on earth, the greatest power that there is to minister to the welfare of mankind; to leave it unprepared and unprotected is not only to disregard the national welfare, but to be no less than guilty of a crime against civilization."

May 30, 1923—*The Price of Freedom* p. 348

"A people who neglect their national defense are putting in jeopardy their national honor."

Annual Message to Congress, December 6, 1923
The Mind of the President p. 232

"I wish crime might be abolished; but I would not therefore abolish courts and police protection. I wish war might be made impossible but I would not leave my country unprotected . . ."

Letter to the National Council for Prevention of War, July 23, 1924
The Mind of the President pp. 235-36

DELEGATION

"It is not sufficient to entrust details to someone else. They must be entrusted to someone who is competent."

Autobiography of Calvin Coolidge p. 196

DEMOCRACY

"There is and can be no doubt of the triumph of democracy in human affairs, than there is of the triumph of gravitation in the physical world; the only question is how and when."

July 4, 1916—*Have Faith in Massachusetts* p. 24

DEMOCRATS

" . . . there were some quarters in the opposing party where it was thought it would be good strategy to encourage my party to nominate me [in 1924], thinking that it would be easy to accomplish my defeat. I do not know whether their judgment was wrong or whether they overdid the operation . . ."

Autobiography of Calvin Coolidge p. 187

DEPRESSION

"If the people have sufficient moderation and contentment to be willing to improve their condition by the process of enlarging production, eliminating waste, and distributing equitably, a prosperity almost without limit lies before us. If the people are to be dominated by selfishness, seeking immediate riches by nonproductive speculation and by wasteful quarreling over the returns from industry, they will be confronted by the inevitable results of depression and privation. If they will continue industrious and thrifty, contented with fair wages and moderate profits, and the returns which accrue from the development of our natural resources, our prosperity will extend itself indefinitely."

Third Annual Message to Congress, December 8, 1925
Messages and Papers of the Presidents p. 9537

"When depression in business comes we begin to be very conservative in our financial affairs. We save our money and take no chances in its investment. Yet in our political actions we go in the opposite direction. We begin to support radical measures and cast our votes for those who advance the most reckless proposals.

"This is a curious and illogical reaction. When times are good we might take a chance on a radical government. But when we are financially weakened we need the soundest and wisest of men and measures."

Calvin Coolidge Says October 7, 1930

"If business can be let alone and assured of reasonable freedom from governmental interference and increased taxes, that will do more than all kinds of legislation to relieve depression. Local governments are justified in spending all the money necessary for direct relief of distress. But the nation and the states will only increase the difficulties by undertaking to restore confidence through legislation. It will be the part of wisdom to give business a free hand to supply its own remedies."

Calvin Coolidge Says October 20, 1930

DEPRESSION, GREAT

"We may say that it was the result of greed and selfishness. But what body is to be specifically charged with that? Were the wage earners too greedy in getting all they could for their work? Were the managers of enterprise, big and little, too greedy in trying to operate at a profit? Were the farmers too greedy in their efforts to make more money by tilling more land and enlarging their production?

"The most we can say is that there has been a general lack of judgment so widespread as to involve practically the whole country. We have learned that we were not so big as we thought we were. We shall have to keep nearer to the ground. We shall not feel so elated, but we shall be much safer."

Quoted in Yankee Magazine, January 1996

DISCIPLINE

"If we did not have the privilege of doing what we wanted to do, we had the much greater benefit of doing what we ought to do."

Autobiography of Calvin Coolidge p. 55

"It broke down our selfishness, it conquered our resistance, it supplanted impulse, and finally it enthroned reason."

Autobiography of Calvin Coolidge p. 55

"We live in an impatient age. We demand results. We find a long and laborious process very irksome, and are constantly seeking for a short cut. But there is no easy method of securing discipline. It is axiomatic that there is no royal road to learning. The effort for discipline must be intensive, and to a considerable degree it must be lifelong. But it is absolutely necessary if there is to be any self-direction or any self-control. The worst evil that could be inflicted upon the youth of the land would be to leave them without restraint and completely at the mercy of their own uncontrolled inclinations. Under such conditions education would be impossible, and all orderly development intellectually or morally would be hopeless. I do not need to picture the result. We know too well what weakness and depravity follow when the ordinary processes of discipline are neglected."

Foundations of the Republic p. 105

DIVERSITY

"It is the natural and correct attitude of mind for each of us to have regard for our own origin. There is abundant room here for the preservation and development of the many divergent virtues that are characteristic of the different races which have made America home. They ought to cling to all these virtues and cultivate them tenaciously."

To immigrants, October 16, 1924
The Mind of the President p. 223

"It is not desirable that we should all attempt to be alike. Progress is not secured through uniformity and similarity but rather multiplicity and diversity. We should all be intent on maintaining our own institutions and customs, preserving the purity of our own language and literature, fostering the ideals of our own culture and society. . . . Instead of considering our variations an obstacle, we ought to realize that they are a contribution to harmonious political and economic relations."

Address before the Pan-American Congress, Havana, January 16, 1928
Messages and Papers of the Presidents p. 9759

DIVIDENDS

"The suspension of one man's dividends is the suspension of another man's pay envelope."

January 7, 1914—*Have Faith in Massachusetts* pp. 3-4

DISARMAMENT

"The theory of the United States is for each nation to defend itself, cultivate friendly relations with others and reduce armaments so that they are not considered a menace anywhere. This theory disarms for security."

Calvin Coolidge Says September 9, 1930

DOGS

"Any man who does not like dogs and want them about does not deserve to be in the White House."

First Dogs p. 3

DUTY

"Duty is not collective; it is personal."

November 1, 1919—*Have Faith in Massachusetts* p. 271

"No man has a right to place his own ease or convenience or the opportunity of making money above his duty to the State."

September 24, 1919—*Have Faith in Massachusetts* p. 227

ECONOMY

"After order and liberty, economy is one of the highest essentials of a free government."

Adequate Brevity p. 33

"I favor the policy of economy, not because I wish to save money, but because I wish to save people. The men and women of this country who toil are the ones who bear the cost of the Government. Every dollar that we carelessly waste means that their life will be so much the more meager. Every dollar that we prudently save means that their life will be so much the more abundant. Economy is idealism in its most practical form."

Inaugural Address, March 4, 1925
The Mind of the President p. 108

"I believe not only in advocating economy in public expenditure, but in its practical application and actual accomplishment."

Calvin Coolidge of Northampton p. 12

"I am for economy. After that I am for more economy."

Foundations of the Republic p. 47

"Economy is the method by which we prepare today to afford the improvements of tomorrow."

> Third Annual Message to Congress, December 8, 1925
> *Messages and Papers of the Presidents* p. 9517

EDUCATION

"My education began with a set of blocks which had on them the Roman numerals and the letters of the alphabet. It is not yet finished."

> *Autobiography of Calvin Coolidge* p. 30

"It is characteristic of the unlearned that they are forever proposing something which is old, and because it has recently come to their attention, supposing it to be new."

> June 25, 1919—*Have Faith in Massachusetts* p. 231

"To a race which claims a heritage of eternity the important question is not where we are but where we are going. Education fails which does not help in furnishing this with some solution. It ought to confer the ability to see in an unfolding history the broadening out of the base of civilization, the continued growth of the power and the dignity of the individual, the enlarging solidarity and stability of society, and the increasing reign of righteousness."

> June 7, 1922—*The Price of Freedom* p. 163

"The great service which education must perform is to confirm our faith in the world, establish our settled convictions, and maintain an open mind. The heritage of all the past is neither mean nor insignificant. It is a high estate."

> June 7, 1922—*The Price of Freedom* p. 169

"Education which is not based on religion and character is not education."

> December 21, 1922—*The Price of Freedom* p. 216

"Education is the process by which each individual recreates his own universe and determines its dimensions."

> June 19, 1923—*The Price of Freedom* p. 381

"Civilization depends not only upon the knowledge of the people, but upon the use they make of it. If knowledge be wrongfully used, civilization commits suicide. . . . Education must give not only power but direction. It must minister to the whole man or it fails."

President Coolidge (Whiting) p. ix

EFFORT

"When industries can be carried on without any struggle, their results will be worthless, and when wages can be secured without effort they will have no purchasing value."

Have Faith in Massachusetts p. 81

FACTORIES

"The man who builds a factory builds a temple, . . . the man who works there worships there, and to each is due, not scorn and blame, but reverence and praise."

February 4, 1916—*Have Faith in Massachusetts* p. 14
Adequate Brevity p. 24

FATE

"Fate bestows its rewards on those who put themselves in the proper attitude to receive them."

Autobiography of Calvin Coolidge p. 180

"We know that only ignorance and superstition seek to explain events by fate and destiny."

Adequate Brevity p. 49

FEDERAL FUNDING

"One insidious practice which sugar-coats the dose of Federal intrusion is the division of expense for public improvements or services between state and national treasuries. The ardent States Rights advocate sees in this practice a vicious weakening of the state system. The extreme federalist is apt to look upon it in cynical fashion as bribing the states into subordination. The average American, believing in our dual-sovereignty system, must feel that the policy of national-doles to the states is bad and may become disastrous. We may go on yet for a time with the easy assumption that 'if the states *will not*, the nation *must*.' But that way lies trouble. When the National Treasury contributes half, there is temptation to extravagance by the state. We have seen some examples in connection with the Federal contributions to road building. Yet there are constant demands for more Federal contributions. Whenever by that plan we take something from one group of states and give it to another group, there is grave danger that we do an economic injustice on one side and a political injury on the other. We impose unfairly on the strength of the strong, and we encourage the weak to indulge their weakness."

Address at Arlington National Cemetery, May 30, 1925
The Mind of the President pp. 68-69
Messages and Papers of the Presidents pp. 9502-03

"The financial programme of the Chief Executive does not contemplate expansion of these subsidies. My policy in this matter is not predicated alone on the drain which these subsidies make on the National Treasury. This of itself is sufficient to cause concern. But I am fearful that this broadening of the field of government activities is detrimental to both the Federal and the state governments. Efficiency of Federal operations is impaired as their scope is duly enlarged. Efficiency of state governments is impaired as they relinquish responsibilities which are rightfully theirs."

At Memorial Continental Hall, January 21, 1924
The Mind of the President p. 73

"Unfortunately the Federal Government has strayed far afield from its legitimate business. It has trespassed upon fields where there should be no trespass. If we could confine our Federal expenditures to the legitimate obligations and functions of the Federal Government, a material reduction would be apparent. But far more important than this would be its effect upon the fabric of our constitutional form of government, which tends to be gradually weakened and undermined by this encroachment. The cure for this is not in our hands. It lies with the people. It will come when they realize the necessity of State assumption of State responsibility. It will come when they realize that the laws under which the Federal Government hands out contributions to the states are placing upon them a double burden of taxation—Federal taxation in the first instance to raise the moneys which the Government donates to the states, and state taxation in the second instance to meet the extravagances of state expenditures which are tempted by Federal donations."

At Memorial Continental Hall, January 21, 1924
The Mind of the President pp. 73-74

"While the amount of money taken annually from the federal Treasury for subsidies to states is not inconsiderable, the dangers inherent in the policy are of greater importance. To relieve the states of their just obligations by resort to the federal Treasury in the final resort is hurtful rather than helpful to the state and unfair to the payers of national taxes. To tempt the states by federal subsidies to sacrifice their vested rights is not a wholesome practice no matter how worthy the object to be attained.

"Federal interference in state functions can never be justified as a permanent continuing policy even if, which is doubtful, such interference is warranted by emergency conditions as a temporary expedient. . . . [W]here once the Government engages in such an enterprise, it is almost impossible to terminate its connection therewith. We should not only decidedly refuse to countenance additional federal participation in state-aid projects, but should make careful study of all our activities of that character with a view to curtailing them."

1927 Budget Message, December 5, 1927
Messages and Papers of the Presidents p. 9720

FEDERALISM

"What we need is not more Federal government, but better local government."

Address at Arlington National Cemetery, May 30, 1925
The Mind of the President p. 68

FISHING

"I have been so busy out at the Lodge catching fish—there are 45,000 out there—I haven't caught them all yet, but I have all pretty well intimidated."

August 7, 1928—*The Talkative President* p. 18

FLAG, UNITED STATES

"It was never flaunted for the glory of royalty, but to be born under it is to be born a child of a king, and to establish a home under it is to be the founder of a royal house."

May 26, 1919—*Have Faith in Massachusetts* p. 177
Adequate Brevity p. 39

"He who lives under it and is loyal to it is loyal to truth and justice everywhere. He who lives under it and is disloyal to it is a traitor to the human race everywhere."

May 26, 1919—*Have Faith in Massachusetts* p. 178

"We do honor to the stars and stripes as the emblem of our country and the symbol of all that our patriotism means.

"We identify the flag with almost everything we hold dear on earth. It represents our peace and security, our civil and political liberty, our freedom of religious worship, our family, our friends, our home. We see it in the great multitude of blessings, of rights and privileges that make up our country.

"But when we look at our flag and behold it emblazoned with all our rights, we must remember that it is equally a symbol of our duties. Every glory that we associate with it is the result of duty done. A yearly contemplation of our flag strengthens and purifies the national conscience."

Source Unknown

FLORIDA

"I haven't visited Florida. I judge from current news reports that Florida is not in need just at the present time of additional guests."

November 3, 1925—*The Talkative President* p. 44

FOREIGN POLICY

"America stands ready to bear its share of the burdens of the world, but it cannot live the life of other peoples, it cannot remove from them the necessity of working out their own destiny. It recognizes their independence and the right to establish their own form of government, but

America will join no nation in destroying what it believes ought to be preserved or in profaning what it believes ought to be held sacred. We are at peace with all peoples."

February 22, 1922—The Price of Freedom p. 148

"It isn't helpful for me to keep talking about certain foreign relations unless there is some development that warrants some statement on my part. I didn't really want to keep rehashing practically the same thing, because it irritates foreign countries oftentimes and they wonder why the White House keeps making statements that don't appear to them to be very helpful."

April 10, 1925—The Talkative President pp. 25-26

"Our Government does not propose, however, to enter into relations with another regime which refuses to recognize the sanctity of international obligations. I do not propose to barter away for the privilege of trade any of the cherished rights of humanity. I do not propose to make merchandise of American principles. These rights and principles must go wherever the sanctions of our Government go."

Annual Message to Congress, December 6, 1923
The Mind of the President p. 45

"While having a due regard for our own affairs, the protection of our own rights, and the advancement of our own people, we can afford to be liberal toward others. Our example has become of great importance in the world. It is recognized that we are independent, detached, and can and do take a disinterested position in relation to international affairs. Our charity embraces the earth. Our trade is far flung. Our financial favors are widespread. Those who are peaceful and law-abiding realize that not only they have nothing to fear from us, but that they can rely on our moral support. Proposals for promoting the peace of the world will have careful consideration. . . . We know that peace comes from honesty and fair dealing, from moderation, and a generous regard for the rights of others. The heart of the Nation is more important than treaties. A spirit of generous consideration is a more certain defense than great armaments."

Fifth Annual Message to Congress, December 6, 1927
Messages and Papers of the Presidents p. 9741

"Nations which are torn by dissension and discord, which are weak and inefficient at home, have little standing or influence abroad. Even the blind do not choose the blind to lead them."

May Day 1927—*Messages and Papers of the Presidents* p. 9702

"We have sufficient reserve resources so that we need not be hasty in asserting our rights. We can afford to let our patience be commensurate with our power."

May Day 1927—*Messages and Papers of the Presidents* p. 9701

"We can best deal with a nation that maintains our standard of living."

Calvin Coolidge Says July 30, 1930

"From the time when President Washington negotiated the Jay Treaty with England up to the present hour, almost every important agreement ratified with a foreign power has been accompanied in this country by bitter criticism of our own government, and wholesale assaults upon the other contracting country. Yet in the light of history, it would be hard to find such an agreement that has not been fairly justified by results. After the bad temper of the period has been dissipated by time and reason, the mutual advantages have been apparent. Our diplomacy has not been inferior. Our statesmen have been able to be just to ourselves and fair to others."

Calvin Coolidge Says September 11, 1930

FORGIVENESS

"There is an obligation to forgive but it does not extend to the unrepentant. To give them aid and comfort is to support their evil doing and to become what is known in law as an accessory after the fact. A government which does that is a reproach to civilization and will soon have on its hands the blood of its citizens."

October 4, 1919—*Have Faith in Massachusetts* p. 247

FREE ENTERPRISE

"I favor the American system of individual enterprise, and I am opposed to any general extension of government ownership, and control."

Calvin Coolidge of Northampton p. 12

FREEDOM

"There is no greater service we can render the oppressed of the earth than to maintain inviolate the freedom of our own citizens."

November 2, 1918—*Have Faith in Massachusetts* p. 154

"There is no substitute for a militant freedom. The only alternative is submission and slavery."

April 27, 1922—*The Price of Freedom* p. 159

GAIN

"There is very little that is really worth while which can be bought or sold. The desire for gain has made many cowards, but it has never made a hero."

Adequate Brevity p. 43

GOVERNMENT

"It is preeminently the province of government to protect the weak."

The Presidency of Calvin Coolidge, p. 175

"Where the people themselves are the government, it needs no argument to demonstrate that what the people cannot do their government cannot do."

April 13, 1923—*The Price of Freedom* p. 292

"There is scarcely a word in the constitution of any of our States or of our nation that was not written there for the purpose of protecting the liberties of the people from some servitude which a despotic government had at some time imposed upon them."

May 30, 1923—*The Price of Freedom,* p. 344

"I would like it if the country could think as little as possible about the Government and give their time and attention more undividedly about the conduct of the private business of the country."

May 1, 1925—*The Talkative President* p. 127

"The United States Government ought to keep from undertaking to transact business that the people themselves ought to transact. It can't function along that line. As soon as the Government tries to transact such business, the people with whom it is being transacted don't regard it as the Government's business. They think it ought not to be done for the benefit of the Government in a way that would be for the benefit of the Treasury or all the people, but that it ought to be done for their benefit. And that always creates a situation that it is extremely difficult to contend with and one which is practically impossible. So that it is my policy, in so far as I can, to keep Government out of business, withdraw from that business that it is engaged in temporarily, and not to be in favor of its embarking on new enterprises."

December 9, 1923—*The Talkative President* p. 137

"Good government cannot be found on the bargain counter. We have seen samples of bargain counter government in the past when low tax rates were secured by increasing the bonded debt for current expenses or refusing to keep our institutions up to the standard in repairs, extensions, equipment, and accommodations. I refuse, and the Republican Party refuses, to endorse that method of sham and shoddy economy."

Coolidge: An American Enigma p. 104

"The age of perfection is still in the somewhat distant future, but it is more in danger of being retarded by mistaken Government activity than it is from lack of legislation."

Third Annual Message to the Congress, December 8, 1925
Messages and Papers of the Presidents p. 9514

"Government should not assume for the people the inevitable burdens of existence."

Adequate Brevity p. 43

"We have had too much government action, with attendant publicity, proposing to cure human illness which no government can cure and too much public opposition when there was nothing to oppose."

Calvin Coolidge Says November 11, 1930

GOVERNMENT AID

"If we give the best that is in us to our private affairs we shall have little need of government aid."

Calvin Coolidge Says November 4, 1930

GOVERNMENT, LOCAL

"The functions which the Congress are to discharge are not those of local government but of national government. The greatest solicitude should be exercised to prevent any encroachment upon the rights of the states or their various political subdivisions. Local self-government is one of our most precious possessions. It is the greatest contributing factor to the stability, strength, liberty, and progress of the nation. It ought not to be infringed by assault or undermined by purchase. It ought not to be abdicate its power through weakness or resign its authority through favor. It does not at all follow that because abuses exist it is the concern of the federal Government to attempt their reform.

"Society is in much more danger from encumbering the national Government beyond its wisdom to comprehend, or its ability to administer, than from leaving the local communities to bear their own burdens and remedy their own evils. Our local habit and custom is so strong, our variety of race and creed is so great, the federal authority is so tenuous, that the area within which it can function successfully is very limited. The wiser policy is to leave the localities, so far as we can, possessed of their own sources of revenue and charged with their own obligations."

Third Annual Message to Congress, December 8, 1925
Messages and Papers of the Presidents pp. 9514-15

GOVERNMENT SPENDING

"Of course, a good many proposals are made by people that have very excellent things that they would like to have the Government do, but they come from people that have no responsibility for providing ways and means by which their proposals can be carried out. I don't think in all my experience, which has been very large with people that come before me in and out of Government with proposals for spending money, I have ever had any proposal from anyone as to what could be done to save any money. Sometimes linked with the proposal for an immediate large expenditure is the suggestion that it ultimately will result in a saving. I think that is about the extent of the outside assistance I have had in that direction."

December 14, 1928—*The Talkative President* p. 112

GREATNESS

"A wholesome regard for the memory of great men of long ago is the best assurance to a people of a continuation of great men to come, who shall still be able to instruct, to lead, and to inspire. A people who worship at the shrine of true greatness will themselves be truly great."

July 6, 1922—*The Price of Freedom* p. 174

"We need never fear that we shall not be called on to do great things in the future if we do small things well at present."

December 21, 1925—*Messages and Papers of the Presidents* p. 9547

"Great men are the ambassadors of Providence sent to reveal to their fellow men their unknown selves. . . . They leave no successor. The heritage of greatness descends to the people."

Adequate Brevity p. 44

"The great man is he who can express the unuttered opinions of his time, direct energy along profitable channels, divine the spirit of the people, and unify action under just and stable institutions of government."

Adequate Brevity p. 44

"There can be no national greatness which does not rest upon the personal integrity of the people."

Adequate Brevity p. 45

GROWTH

"All growth depends upon activity. Life is manifest only by action. There is no development physically or intellectually without effort, and effort means work."

Adequate Brevity p. 45

HISTORY

"Savages have no history."

July 4, 1916—*Have Faith in Massachusetts* p. 21

HOME OWNERSHIP

"The moral power of the nation rests on the home, the schoolhouse, and the place of worship. The government looks after education and few churches are overcrowded. But home owners are too few."

Calvin Coolidge Says July 21, 1930

HUMOR

"I very soon learned that making fun of people in a public way was not a good method to secure friends, or likely to lead to much advancement, and I have scrupulously avoided it."

Autobiography of Calvin Coolidge p. 71

HUNTING

"I think the idea that I might go hunting in Kentucky arose from the fact that the bird dog that was given to me in Superior [Wisconsin] I had Colonel Starling send down to a friend of his in Kentucky, who is a very fine trainer of dogs. I presume that all the hunting I will do in Kentucky will be done by proxy through this dog."

September 14, 1928—*The Talkative President* p. 18

IDEAS

"It is the ferment of ideas, the clash of disagreeing judgments, the privilege of the individual to develop his own thought and shape his own character which makes progress possible."

1925

IDLENESS

"It is not industry, but idleness, that is degrading."

Autobiography of Calvin Coolidge p. 68

INDEPENDENCE

"There is no dignity quite so impressive, and no one independence quite so important, as living within your means."

Autobiography of Calvin Coolidge p. 159

INFLATION

"Inflation is repudiation."

January 11, 1922—*The Price of Freedom* p. 110

IMMIGRATION

"Restricted immigration is not an offensive but purely a defensive action. It is not adopted in criticism of others in the slightest degree, but solely for the purpose of protecting ourselves. We cast no aspersions on any race or creed, but we must remember that every object of our institutions of society and government will fail unless America be kept American."

Accepting the Republican presidential nomination, August 14, 1924
The Mind of the President pp. 216-17

"We ought to have no prejudice against an alien because he is an alien. The standard which we apply to our inhabitants is that of manhood, not place of birth. Restrictive immigration is to a large degree for economic purposes. It is applied in order that we may not have a larger annual increment of good people within our borders that we can weave into our economic fabric in such a way as to supply their needs without undue injury to ourselves."

Third Annual Message to Congress, December 8, 1925
Messages and Papers of the Presidents p. 9526

"Those who do not want to be partakers of the American spirit out not to settle in America."

Adequate Brevity p. 50

"We are all agreed, whether we be Americans of the first or of the seventh generation on this soil, that is not desirable to receive more immigrants than can reasonably be assured of bettering their condition by coming here. For the sake both of those who would come and more especially of those already here, it has been thought wise to avoid the danger of increasing our numbers too fast. It is not a reflection on any race or creed. We might not be able to support them if their numbers were too great. In such event, the first sufferers would be the most recent immigrants, unaccustomed to our life and language and industrial methods. We want to keep wages and living conditions good for everyone who is now here or who may come here.

"As a nation, our first duty must be those who are already our inhabitants, whether native or immigrants."

To immigrants, October 16, 1924
The Mind of the President p. 222

"We have certain standards of life that we believe are best for us. We do not ask other nations to discard theirs, but we do wish to preserve ours. Standards, government and culture under our free institutions are not so much a matter of constitutions and laws as of public opinion, ways of thought and methods of life of the people. We reflect on no one in wanting immigrants who will be assimilated into our ways of thinking and living. Believing we can best serve the world in that way, we restrict immigration."

Calvin Coolidge Says December 13, 1930

INTEGRITY

"The can be no national greatness which does not rest upon the personal integrity of the people."

Source Unknown

INVESTMENT, OVERSEAS

"Much of the criticism of the starting of foreign branches by our industries is short sighted. All the business on earth cannot be done within the confines of the United States. One disadvantage in world trade is the lower standards of living in other countries. Foreign branches will carry our methods and standards, which will be contagious. Pressure of low standard production will be reduced. International finance will be more stable.

"Usually foreign branches will use our machinery and raw materials and increase local prosperity. That will make customers who are better able to absorb our exports. Meantime the tariff gives the advantage in our markets to domestic producers.

"The problem has a broader aspect. It is our duty to take care of our own people. That we can do. But a backward, undeveloped world instead of being a help is a menace. Peace requires arrangements by which other people can prosper. It is our duty to contribute of our capital and our skill to that prosperity. Such a course in the end will provide more employment, increase our material welfare and give us the satisfaction of having borne our part of the burden of civilization."

Calvin Coolidge Says November 12, 1930

JUSTICE

"Let justice and the economic laws be applied to the strong; but for the weak there must be mercy and charity; not the gratuity which pauperizes, but the assistance which restores. That too, is justice."

Adequate Brevity p. 53

LABOR LEGISLATION

"Workmen's compensation, hours and conditions of labor are cold consolation, if there be no employment."

September 1, 1919—*Have Faith in Massachusetts* pp. 201-02

LANGUAGE, FOUL

"An evil tongue cannot have a pure mind. We read that 'out of the abundance of the heart the mouth speaketh.' This is a truth which is worthy of much thought. He who gives license to his tongue only discloses the contents of his mind. By the excess of his words he proclaims his lack of discipline. By his very violence he shows his weakness. The youth or man who by disregarding this principle thinks he is displaying his determination and resolution and emphasizing his statements is in reality only revealing an intellectual poverty, a deficiency in self-control and self-respect, a want of accurate thinking and of spiritual insight, which cannot come save from a reverence for the truth. There are no human actions which are unimportant, none to which we can be indifferent. All of them lead either towards destruction and death, or towards construction and life."

Foundations of the Republic pp. 104-05

LAW

"Men do not make laws. They do but discover them. Laws must be justified by something more than the will of the majority. They must rest on the eternal foundation of righteousness."

January 7, 1914—*Have Faith in Massachusetts* p. 4

"Authority and sanctity of the law. When that goes all goes. It costs something but it is the cheapest thing that can be bought; it causes some inconvenience but it is the foundation of all convenience, the orderly execution of the laws."

October 4, 1919—*Law and Order* p. 24

"While there may be those of high intelligence who violate the law at times, the barbarian and the defective always violate it."

Inaugural Address, March 4, 1925
Messages and Papers of the Presidents p. 9488

"Things are so ordered in this world that those who violate its law cannot escape the penalty. Nature is inexorable. If men do not follow the truth they cannot live."

Autobiography of Calvin Coolidge p. 51

"I do not feel that any one ever really masters the law, but it is not difficult to master the approaches to the law . . ."

Autobiography of Calvin Coolidge p. 76

"Those who attend a law school know how to pass the examinations, while those who study in an office know how to apply their knowledge to actual practice."

Autobiography of Calvin Coolidge p. 83

"Laws do not make reforms, reforms make laws."

Have Faith in Massachusetts p. 83
Adequate Brevity p. 55

"When I was admitted to practice . . . the law still occupied the high position of a profession. It had then not assumed any of its later aspects of a trade."

Autobiography of Calvin Coolidge p. 84

"My heart was in the law."

Autobiography of Calvin Coolidge p. 101

"The difference between despotism and democracy is not a difference in the requirement of obedience, it is a difference in rulers. He becomes an absolute sovereign by absolute obedience. He will be a limited sovereign if he limits his obedience. The criminal loses all his freedoms. It is easy to see that democracy will have obtained perfection when laws are made wholly wise and obedience is made wholly complete."

The Price of Freedom p. 188

"Real reform does not begin with a law, it ends with a law. The attempt to dragoon the body when the need is to convince the soul will end only in revolt."

August 10, 1922—*The Price of Freedom* p. 206
Adequate Brevity p. 87

"Disobedience to it is disobedience to the people."

October 4, 1919—*Law and Order* p. 24

"The choice lies between living under coercion and intimidation, the forces of evil, or under the laws of the people, orderly, speaking their settled convictions, the revelation of a divine authority."

October 4, 1919—*Law and Order* p. 25

"There are strident voices urging resistance to law in the name of freedom. They are not seeking freedom even for themselves—they have it; they are seeking to enslave others. Their works are evil."

January 8, 1920—Law and Order p. 57

"Laws are not manufactured, they are not imposed; they are rules of action existing from everlasting to everlasting. He who resists them resists himself; he commits suicide."

January 8, 1920—Law and Order p. 58

"One with the law is a majority."

Accepting the Republican vice-presidential nomination at
Northampton, Massachusetts, July 27, 1920

"The law represents the voice of the people. Behind it, and supporting it, is a divine sanction. Enforcement of law and obedience to law, by the very nature of our institutions, are not matters of choice in this republic, but the expression of a mortal requirement of living in accordance with the truth. They are clothed with a spiritual significance, in which is revealed the life or the death of the American ideal of self-government."

Annual Message to Congress, December 6, 1923
The Mind of the President p. 241

"New activities require new laws."

Address to the Pan-American Congress, Havana, January 16, 1928
Messages and Papers of the Presidents p. 9761

"It is the mind behind the law that makes it truly effective. Laws are insufficient to endow a nation with righteousness."

Adequate Brevity p. 42

"The law, changed and changeable on slight provocation, loses its sanctity and authority."

Adequate Brevity p. 54

LEADERSHIP

"Men do what I tell them to do—why, is a great mystery to me."

Your Son Calvin Coolidge June 25, 1918

LEARNING

"There have been great men with little of what we call education. There have been small men with a great deal of learning. There has never been a great people who did not possess great learning."

Adequate Brevity p. 59

LEGISLATION

"The people cannot look to legislation generally for success."

January 7, 1914—*Have Faith in Massachusetts* p. 5

"Don't hurry to legislate. Give administration a chance to catch up with legislation."

January 7, 1914—*Have Faith in Massachusetts* p. 8
Adequate Brevity p 57

"There can be no perfect control of personal conduct by national legislation."

August 10, 1922—*The Price of Freedom* p. 204

"You can display no greater wisdom than by resisting proposals for needless legislation."

January 8, 1920—*Law and Order* p. 47

"It is much more important to kill bad bills than to pass good ones."

Your Son Calvin Coolidge September 6, 1910

"Unsound economic conditions are not conducive to sound legislation."

Adequate Brevity p. 57

"We have had too much legislating by clamor, by tumult, by pressure. Representative government ceases when outside influence of any kind is substituted for the judgment of the representative. This does not mean that the opinion of constituents is to be ignored. It is to be weighed most carefully, for the representative must represent; but his oath provides that it must be 'faithfully and impartially according to the best of his abilities and understanding, agreeably to the rules and regulations of the Constitution and the laws.' Opinions and instructions do not outmatch the Constitution. Against it they are void. It is an insult to any . . . constituency to suggest that they were so intended. Instructions are not given unless given constitutionally. There can be no constitutional instruction to do an unconstitutional act."

May 6, 1920—Law and Order p. 42
Adequate Brevity p. 89

"A large part of the history of free institutions is the history of the people struggling to emancipate themselves from unrestricted legislation."

Adequate Brevity p. 56

LIBERTY

"Liberty can only be secured by obedience to the law."

November 4, 1919—Have Faith in Massachusetts, p. 262

"It is the abuse of liberty which warrants oppression."

April 18, 1923—The Price of Freedom p. 327

"It is senseless to boast of our liberty when we find that to so shocking an extent it is merely the liberty to go ill-governed."

Address at Arlington National Cemetery, May 30, 1925
The Mind of the President p. 70

LITIGATION

"No litigant should be required to submit his case to the hazard and expense of a political campaign."

January 7, 1914—Have Faith in Massachusetts p. 5

LUCK

"There are people who complain that they do not have any luck. These are the opportunists who think their destiny is all shaped outside themselves. They are always waiting for something to happen. Not only is nothing very good likely to happen to this class, but if some fortune seems to come it tends to turn out disastrously. They are usually ruined by success.

"Our real luck lies within ourselves. It is a question of character. It depends on whether we follow the inward light of conscience. Such men rise above the realm of temporary circumstance. They are great even in defeat.

"Napoleon followed his star, seeking luck outside himself, was great only in victory. But in Egypt, at Moscow, at Waterloo, his glory departed. General Lee, sacrificing himself for what he felt was his duty, was no less great after Appomattox. Poverty, obscurity, assassination, only revealed the greatness of Lincoln. The wrath of man praised him. If we cannot control our environment, we can control ourselves and our destiny. The man who is right makes his own luck."

Calvin Coolidge Says August 29, 1930

MAN

"No man was ever meanly born. About his cradle is the wondrous miracle of life. He may descend into the depths, he may live in infamy and perish miserably, but he is born great."

January 23, 1921—*The Price of Freedom* p. 17

MASSACHUSETTS

"Have faith in Massachusetts. In some unimportant detail some other States may surpass her, but in general results, there is no place on earth where the people secure, in a larger measure, the blessings of organized government, and nowhere can these functions more properly be termed self-government."

January 7, 1914—*Have Faith in Massachusetts* p. 7

MATERIALISM

"If material rewards be the only measure of success, there is no hope of a peaceful solution of our social questions, for they will never be large enough to satisfy. But such is not the case. Men struggle for material success because that is the path, the process, to the development of character. We ought to demand economic justice, but most of all because it is justice. We must forever realize that material rewards are limited and in a sense they are only incidental and is the only essential. The measure of success is not the quantity of merchandise, but the quality of manhood which is produced."

Coolidge: An American Enigma p. 120

MILITARY MENTALITY

"I find in my own case that my privileges of free speech are a good deal curtailed, because I am President. I think that rule might be taken to heart by the military men of the country. I don't think there is any reason for taking seriously any suggestion that the country at the present time is in danger of being attacked. I know very well that we do not harbor any intention of attacking anyone else. But I suppose that those who have on them the burden of national defense naturally dwell on it, amplify it, enlarge it, and emphasize it. I don't know that they would be of very much value to the country if that wasn't the case. But I do not agree with the methods that they sometimes employ. I don't see why the press should take them very seriously."

January 24, 1928—*The Talkative President* pp. 169-70

MILITARY PREPAREDNESS

"I am not unfamiliar with the claim that if only we had a sufficient military establishment no one would ever molest us. I know of no nation in history that has ever been able to attain that position. I see no reason to expect that we would be the exception."

Address to graduating class of Annapolis, June 3, 1925
The Mind of the President p. 52

MILITARY SPENDING

"You gentlemen are all familiar with the military policy. It seems to be the classic one of securing an appropriation for either the Army or the Navy.

The policy doesn't have very much effect around this office, nor I assume on the Congress, suggesting that our Army is running down in materials and personnel, and that the Navy is just ready to drop into the sea."

September 16, 1924—*The Talkative President* pp. 153-54

"Navy yards, you know, really ought to be for the benefit of the Navy and the country. Yet they are generally considered to be for the benefit of the locality in which they are located."

February 15, 1929—*The Talkative President* p. 173

MODERN ART

"Not long ago, I happened to visit an exhibition of modern pictures. It was held in Pittsburgh, and almost every European nation was represented— [the United Kingdom], France, Germany. Italy—the whole lot of them. And as I looked at those pictures, I felt that I could see through them, into the minds of the nations which had created hem. I could see the torment out of which they had been born. If that nation's psychology was still diseased, so was its art. The traces of neurosis were unmistakable. If, on the other hand, the nation was on the road to recovery, if its people were rediscovering the happiness which they had lost, the story was told in the picture, too."

To English author Beverly Nichols
The Real Calvin Coolidge pp. 115-16

MORAL STANDARDS

"There is no moral standard so high that the people cannot be raised up to it."

February 12, 1922—*The Price of Freedom* p. 131

MORALITY

"If we are too weak to take charge of our own morality, we shall not be strong enough to take charge of our own liberty."

Address at Arlington National Cemetery, May 30, 1925
The Mind of the President p. 71

"Disintegration begins within. We are the possessors of tremendous power, both as individuals and as states. The great question of our institutions is a moral question. Shall we use our power for self-aggrandizement or for service? It has been lack of moral fibre which has been the downfall of the peoples of the past."

To the Vermont Historical Society, Montpelier, January 18, 1921

"A nation that is morally dead will soon be financially dead."

Adequate Brevity p. 96

MOTHER (COOLIDGE'S)

"Whatever was grand and beautiful in form and color attracted her. It seemed as though the rich green tints of the foliage and the blossoms of the flowers came for her in the springtime, and in the autumn, it was for her that the mountain sides were struck with crimson and gold."

Autobiography of Calvin Coolidge p. 13

NATURAL DISASTERS

"For some reason difficult to explain a sudden [natural] disaster . . . , entirely beyond human control, moves people to compassion while they are more or less indifferent to the slaughter of three thousand tribesmen around Mount Ararat and to a far greater loss of life and property in China through deliberate human action by war and resulting famine. With all our civilization, all our humanity, all our religion, men are still less in danger from the elements than they are from each other."

Calvin Coolidge Says September 5, 1930

NEEDS

"We do not need more material development, we need more spiritual development, we do not need more intellectual power, we need more moral power. We do not need more knowledge, we need more character. We do not need more government, we need more culture. We do not need more laws, we need more religion. We do not need more of the things that are seen, we need more of the things that are unseen."

Commencement Address at Wheaton College, June 17, 1921
Calvin Coolidge: Man From Vermont p. 298

NEW YEAR'S RESOLUTIONS

"Perhaps the best resolve is to live so that next year's new resolutions will be unnecessary."

Calvin Coolidge Says December 30, 1930

OBVIOUS, THE

"They criticize me for harping on the obvious . . . . If all the folks in the United States would do the few simple things they know they ought to do, most of our big problems would take care of themselves."

To author Bruce Barton, *Meet Calvin Coolidge* p. 191

OFFICE, PUBLIC

"Our country has maintained the principle that our Government is established for something higher and finer than to permit those who are charged with the responsibility of office, or any class whose favor they might seek, to get what they can get out of it."

Adequate Brevity p. 74

"The Government of the United States is not for the gratification of the people who happen to hold office. It is established to promote the general welfare of all the people. That is the American ideal. No matter how many officeholders there may be, or what their origin, our institutions are a failure unless they serve all the citizens in their own homes. It is always necessary to find out what effect the institutions of Government and society have on the wage earner, in order to judge the disability of their continuance."

Foundations of the Republic p. 77

PARLIAMENTARY SYSTEM (CONTRAST WITH)

"We often have Governors and occasionally a President without a legislative majority in their party. But even that is better for us than constant uncertainty and perpetual turmoil of elections. We know fairly well what to expect from government for the next two years. Our system may not be so responsive but it is safe. If we do not get what we want we probably get more of what we ought to have."

Calvin Coolidge Says December 8, 1930

PATRIOTISM

"Patriotism is easy to understand in America. It means looking out for yourself by looking out for your country. In no other nation on earth does this principle have such complete application."

May 30, 1923—*The Price of Freedom* p. 333

"Patriotism does not mean a regard for some special section or an attachment for some special interest, and a narrow prejudice against other sections and other interests; it means a love of the whole country."

May 30, 1923—*The Price of Freedom* p. 348

"Not to know and appreciate the many excellent qualities of our own country constitutes an intellectual poverty which instead of being displayed with pride ought to be acknowledged with shame."

May Day 1927—*Messages and Papers of the Presidents* p. 9701

"We must eternally smite the rock of public conscience if the waters of patriotism are to pour forth. We must ever be ready to point out the success of our country as justification of our determination to support it."

Adequate Brevity p. 73

"Patriotism can neither be bought or sold. It is not hire and salary. It is not material, but spiritual. It is one of the highest human virtues. To attempt to pay money for it is to offer it an unworthy indignity which cheapens, debases and destroys it."

Adequate Brevity p. 74

PAST, THE

"To honor the past, is to render more secure the present."

Adequate Brevity p. 47

PEACE

"What America should have required was not the keeping of the peace, but the keeping of the soul. . . . Nathan Hale and Joseph Warren did not keep the peace. Nor did Washington and Lincoln. But they kept the faith."

The Preparation of Calvin Coolidge p. 183

"There is another element, more important than all, without which there can not be the slightest hope of a permanent peace. That element lies in the heart of humanity. Unless the desire for peace be cherished there, unless this fundamental and only natural source of brotherly love be cultivated to its highest degree, all artificial efforts will be in vain. Peace will come when there is realization that only under a reign of law, based on righteousness and supported by the religious conviction of the brotherhood of man, can there be any hope of a complete and satisfying life. Parchment will fail, the sword will fail, it is only the spiritual nature of man that can be triumphant."

Inaugural Address, March 4, 1925
Messages and Papers of the Presidents p. 9484

"Having met our war obligation to pay, let us meet our peace obligation to save."

January 8, 1920—*Law and Order* p. 49

"Peace requires arrangements by which other people can prosper."

Calvin Coolidge Says November 12, 1930

"I do not claim to be able to announce any formula that will guarantee the peace of the world."

Adequate Brevity p. 74

"Past wars and national defense cost a very large sum. It pays to be at peace."

Calvin Coolidge Says December 4, 1930

PEOPLE

"This world is made up of all kinds of people. Some are good, and some are better, while others have made it necessary for the government to take charge of them."

Calvin Coolidge Says July 18, 1930

PEOPLE, THE

"Of course it would be folly to argue that the people cannot make political mistakes. They can and do make grave mistakes. They know it, they pay the penalty, but compared with the mistakes which have been made by every kind of autocracy they are unimportant."

Adequate Brevity p. 76

PERSISTENCE

"Nothing in the world can take the place of persistence. Talent will not; nothing is more common than unsuccessful men with talent. Genius will not; unrewarded genius is almost a proverb. Education will not; the world is full of educated derelicts. Persistence and determination alone are omnipotent. The slogan 'Press On' has solved and always will solve the problems of the human race."

1932

POLITICAL MIND

"The political mind is the product of men in public life who have been twice spoiled. They have been spoiled with praise and they have been spoiled with abuse."

Autobiography of Calvin Coolidge p. 229

POLITICS

"There is only one form of political strategy in which I have any confidence, and that is to try to do the right thing and sometimes to succeed."

Autobiography of Calvin Coolidge p. 188

"At least 400 Democrats voted for me [for mayor]. Their leaders can't see why. I know why. They knew I had done things for them, bless their honest Irish hearts."

Your Son Calvin Coolidge December 10, 1909

"We need more of the Office Desk and less of the Show Window in politics. Let men in office substitute the midnight oil for the limelight."

September 1916—*Have Faith in Massachusetts* p. 46

"Talking is all right, but the side that organizes and gets the vote to the polls is the side that wins."

To Everett Sanders, September 21, 1932, *Meet Calvin Coolidge* p. 202

"It is much better not to press a candidacy too much, but to let it develop on its own merits without artificial stimulation. If the people want a man they will nominate him, if they do not want him he had best let the nomination go to another."

Autobiography of Calvin Coolidge pp. 121-22

"So much emphasis has been put upon the false that the significance of the true has been obscured and politics has come to convey the meaning of crafty and cunning selfishness, instead of candid and sincere service."

Adequate Brevity p. 77

"Politics is not an end, but a means. It is not a product, but a process. It is the art of government. Like other values it has its counterfeits. So much emphasis has been placed upon the false that the significance of the true has been obscured and politics has come to convey the meaning of crafty and cunning selfishness, instead of candid and sincere service. The Greek definition shows a nobler purpose. *Politikos* means city-rearing, statecraft. And when we remember that city also meant civilization, the spurious presentment, mean and sordid, drops away and the real figure of the politician, dignified and honorable, a minister to civilization, author and finisher of government, is revealed in its true and dignified proportions."

President Coolidge (Whiting), p. x

"We have in this country a certain type of officeholder, fortunately not large, who are always out with square and compass seeking to find out what the political effect will be of every action they take. They do not need to make such elaborate investigations. Any one with a little experience can tell them in advance that the effect of action based on such motives will always be bad. All the predominant political opinion of the nation which is worth cultivating is never impressed by decisions made for effect. Those who compose that body want responsible officeholders to try to find out what is best for the welfare of the people and do that. They are moved by sincerity and integrity of purpose. Pretense does not appeal to them.

"That is the reason why those who seek popularity so seldom find it, while those who follow an informed conscience so often are astonished by a wide public approval. The people know a sham even when they seem to be trying to fool themselves and they cannot help having a wholesome respect for a reality. The best political effect usually comes to those who disregard it."

Calvin Coolidge Says October 15, 1930

POLITICAL PARTIES

"Since its very outset, it has been found necessary to conduct our Government by means of political parties. That system would not have survived from generation to generation if it had not been fundamentally sound and provided the best instrumentalities for the most complete expression of the popular will. It is not necessary to claim that it has always worked perfectly. It is enough to know that nothing better has been devised."

Inaugural Address, March 4, 1925

"Unless those who are elected under the same party designation are willing to assume sufficient responsibility and exhibit sufficient loyalty and coherence, so that they can cooperate with each other in the support of the broad general principles, of the party platform, the election is merely a mockery, no decision is made at the polls, and there is no representation of the popular will."

Inaugural Address, March 4, 1925

"Parties do not maintain themselves. They are maintained by effort. The government is not self-existent. It is maintained by the effort of those who believe in it. The people of America believe in American institutions, the American form of government and the American method of transacting business."

Before the Republican Commercial 'Travelers' Club,
Boston, Massachusetts, April 10, 1920

"As a matter of fact all the political parties are progressive. I can't conceive of a party existing for any length of time that wasn't progressive, or of leadership being effective that wasn't progressive."

The Talkative President p. 9

POLITICAL PARTY CHAIRMEN

"The popular diversion exhibited in the sport world of killing the umpire and taking out the pitcher, when transferred to the political world becomes the demand for the resignation of the party chairman."

Calvin Coolidge Says November 15, 1930

PORK

"The people who start to elect a man to get what he can for his district will probably find they have elected a man who will get what he can for himself."

Have Faith in Massachusetts p. 79

PRESIDENCY

"It has become the custom in our country to expect all Chief Executives, from the President down, to conduct activities analogous to an entertainment bureau."

Autobiography of Calvin Coolidge p. 118

"It is a great advantage to a President, and a major source of safety to the country, for him to know he is not a great man."

Autobiography of Calvin Coolidge p. 173

"The words of the President have an enormous weight and ought not to be used indiscriminately."

Autobiography of Calvin Coolidge p. 195

"Like the glory of a morning sunrise, it can only be experienced—it can not be told."

Autobiography of Calvin Coolidge p. 195

"In the discharge of the duties of the office there is one of action more important than all others. It consists in never doing anything that some one else can do for you."

Autobiography of Calvin Coolidge p. 196

"When I was Mayor of Northampton, I was pretty busy most of the time, and I don't seem to be much busier here. I just have to settle different kinds of things."

Meet Calvin Coolidge p. 106

"I do not choose to run for President in nineteen twenty-eight."

August 2, 1927, Rapid City, SD—*The Quiet President* p. 384

"We draw our Presidents from the people. It is a wholesome thing for them to return to the people. I came from them. I wish to be one of them again."

Autobiography of Calvin Coolidge p. 242

"The president shouldn't do too much, and he shouldn't know too much. The president can't resign . . . So I constantly said to my cabinet: 'There are many things you gentlemen must not tell me. If you blunder, you can leave, or I can invite you to leave. But if you draw me into all our departmental decisions and something goes wrong, I must stay here, and by involving me, you have lowered the faith of the people in their government.'"

Quoted in *Yankee Magazine*, January 1996

"It costs a great deal to be President."

Autobiography of Calvin Coolidge p. 192

"I hope you all enjoyed your stay over in Vermont. I find it helpful for me to go back once in a while to see that I am not forgetting how people earn their living, how they are required to live, and what happens when those who have harness breaks, or one of their shoes need some repairing, sit down and mend it. You can go out and do some work on fence, do such odd jobs as are necessary to keep the house in repair, and in general do such things as are necessary for the ordinary American citizen to do. There is always a little danger that those who are entrusted with the great responsibilities of business and Government may come to forget about those things and disregard them and lose the point of view of the great bulk of citizens of the country who have to earn their living and are mainly responsible for keeping their houses, farms and shops in repair and maintaining them as a going concern. I find it very helpful to go back and revive my information about those things, lest I should be forgetful about it and get out of sympathy with those who have to carry on the work of the nation."

August 10, 1926—*The Talkative President* pp. 46-47

"It carries sufficient power within itself, so that it does not require any of the outward trappings of pomp and splendor for the purpose of creating an impression. It has a dignity of its own which makes it self-sufficient. Of course, there should be proper formality, and personal relations should be conducted at all times with decorum and dignity, and in accordance with the best traditions of polite society. But there is no need of theatricals."

Autobiography of Calvin Coolidge, p. 216

PRESS, THE

"Whenever any section of our press turns on America and on American institutions, and assumes a foreign attitude, every informed person knows it has fallen from the high estate which is our common heritage, and becoming no longer worthy of regard is destined to defeat and failure. No American can profit by selling his own country for foreign favor."

April 25, 1927—*Messages and Papers of the Presidents* p. 9689

"I have often said that there was no cause for feeling disturbed at being misrepresented in the press. It would be only when they began to say things detrimental to me which were true that I should feel alarm."

Autobiography of Calvin Coolidge p. 184

"One newspaper is better than many criminal laws."

Adequate Brevity p. 78

"They have undertaken to endow me with some characteristics and traits that I didn't altogether know I had. But I have done the best I could do to be perfectly fair with them and, in public, to live up to those traits. I have sometimes found it a little difficult, especially under the provocation that arises out of some of the things that I read in the newspapers, but I have been able to contain myself on those occasions."

To the Gridiron Club Dinner, Washington, D.C., December 1923
Meet Calvin Coolidge pp. 8-9

"An American press which has all the privileges which it enjoys under our institutions, and which derives its support from the progress and well-being of our people, ought to be first and thoroughly American."

April 25, 1927—*Messages and Papers of the Presidents* p. 9691

"Like almost anything else, the standards of the press are ultimately set by the people themselves."

Calvin Coolidge Says October 18, 1930

PRICE CONTROLS

"Government price fixing, once started, has alike no justice and no end. It is an economic folly from which this country has every right to be spared."

McNary-Haugen Farm Relief Bill Veto Message, February 25, 1927
Messages and Papers of the Presidents p. 9660

"Fiat prices match the folly of fiat money."

McNary-Haugen Farm Relief Bill Veto Message, May 23, 1928,
1927 *Messages and Papers of the Presidents* p. 9779

"It is not possible to repeal the law of supply and demand, of cause and effect, or of action and reaction. Value is a matter of opinion. An act of Congress has small jurisdiction over what men think."

Calvin Coolidge Says July 29, 1930

PRIDE

"The mighty in their pride walk alone to destruction."

May 6, 1919—*Have Faith in Massachusetts* p. 177

PRINCIPLES

"Some principles are so constant and so obvious that we do not need to change them, but we need rather to observe them."

Foundations of the Republic p. 52

PRINCIPLES OF THE FOUNDING FATHERS

"These principles there laid down with so much solemnity have now the same binding force as in those revolutionary days when they were recognized and proclaimed. I am not unaware that they are old. Whatever is, is old. It is but our own poor apprehension of it which is new."

June 19, 1919—*Have Faith in Massachusetts* p. 190

PRIVATE PROPERTY

"It is very difficult to reconcile the American ideal of a sovereign people capable of owning and managing their own government with an inability to own and manage their own business."

At Philadelphia, September 25, 1924
The Mind of the President p. 161

PROFITS

"Large profits mean large pay rolls."

January 7, 1914—*Have Faith in Massachusetts* p. 7

"Civilization and profits go hand in hand."

November 27, 1920—*The Price of Freedom* p. 5
Adequate Brevity p. 20

"There is just one condition on which men can secure employment and a living, nourishing, profitable wage, for whatever they contribute to the enterprise, be it labor or capital, and that condition is that some one make a profit of it. That is the sound basis for distribution of wealth and the only one. It cannot be done by law, it cannot be done by public ownership, it cannot be done by socialism. When you deny the right to a profit, you deny the right of a reward to thrift and industry."

December 15, 1916—Law and Order p. 32

"There is just one condition on which men can secure employment and a living, nourishing, profitable wage, for whatever they contribute to the enterprise, be it labor or capital, and that condition is that some one make a profit by it."

Adequate Brevity p. 51

PROPERTY

"All owners of property are charged with a service. These rights and duties have been revealed, through the conscience of society, to have a divine sanction. The very stability of our society rests upon production and conservation. For individuals or for governments to waste and squander their resources is to deny these rights and disregard these obligations. The result of economic dissipation to a nation is always moral decay."

Inaugural Address, March 4, 1925

"The property of the country belongs to the people of the country. Their title is absolute. They do not support any privileged class; they do not need to maintain great military forces; they ought not to be burdened with a great array of public employees."

Inaugural Address, March 4, 1925

"Coincident with the right of individual property under the provisions of our Government is the right of individual property. . . . When once the right of the individual to liberty and equality is admitted, there is no escape from the conclusion that he alone is entitled to the rewards of his own industry. Any other conclusion would necessarily imply either privilege or servitude."

Foundations of the Republic pp. 108-09

"When service is performed, the individual performing it is entitled to the compensation for it. His creation becomes a part of himself. It is his property. To attempt to deal with persons or with property in a communistic or socialistic way is to deny what seems to be this plain fact."

Foundations of the Republic p. 109

PROPERTY RIGHTS

"Ultimately, property rights and personal rights are the same thing."

January 7, 1914—*Have Faith in Massachusetts* p. 6

"We need not concern ourselves much about the rights of property if we will faithfully observe the rights of persons. Under our institutions their rights are supreme. It is not property but the right to hold property, both great and small, which our Constitution guarantees."

Inaugural Address, March 4, 1925

PROSPERITY

"Prosperity is only an instrument to be used, not a deity to be worshipped."

Source Unknown

" . . . we have had many attempts at regulation of industrial activity by law. Some of it has proceeded on the theory that if those who enjoyed material prosperity used it for wrong proposes, such prosperity should be limited or abolished. That is as sound as it would be to abolish writing to prevent forgery."

December 15, 1916—*Have Faith in Massachusetts* p. 65

"If you can base the economic condition of the people on their appearance, the way they are dressed, the general appearance of prosperity, I should say that it was very good. I don't know that that has any significance now, but I noticed most of the ladies had on silk dresses and I thought I saw a rather general display of silk stockings."

June 9, 1925—*The Talkative President* p. 128

"Prosperity does not result from cheap goods but from fair profits."

Calvin Coolidge Says August 27, 1930

PROTECTIONISM

"My observation of protectionism is that it has been successful in practice, however unsound it may appear to be in theory. That must mean the theories have not taken account of all the facts."

Correspondence to Dwight Morrow, March 10, 1920

The Quiet President p. 103

"For over a generation each protective tariff has changed the basis but enlarged the market for imports. Of course, some lines may have been injured and others compelled to come in on a rate more fair to the United States standards of wages and living. That is not saying the new tariffs promoted or retarded the increases. But the fact is higher rates did not decrease the former imports. The most reasonable explanation seems to be that protection encouraged business and a more prosperous people bought more goods abroad. Instead of being disturbed at the tariff foreign nations should know that our general imports will be large so long as our business is good."

Calvin Coolidge Says July 11, 1930

"A very bad tariff would be better than constant agitation, uncertainty, foreign animosity and change. . . . Hope for a purely scientific tariff will prove a delusion. Any prolonged investigations, covering many schedules for the purpose of rewriting the law, will do more harm than good. Many will be injured while none will be satisfied. And the country will not be benefited."

Calvin Coolidge Says September 10, 1930

"We wish to protect our own wage earners, our agriculture and industry from the results of dumping produce on our markets at a price with which they could not compete. But the policy has a deeper significance than that. We are unwilling to profit by the distress of foreign people. We do not want their blood money. Our efforts are not only to protect our own people from cheap goods, which President McKinley said meant cheap men, but we propose to set up a standard that will discourage other nations from exploiting their people by producing cheap goods. Our policy requires fair wages for both domestic and foreign production. We have no market for blood and tears."

Calvin Coolidge Says November 26, 1930

" . . . one of the most wholesome of all means of raising revenue, for it is voluntary in effect, and taxes consumption rather than production."

Vice-Presidential acceptance address, July 27, 1920

PUERTO RICO

"I suggested to them also the great desirability of a general knowledge on the Island of the English language. They are under an English speaking government and are a part of the territory of an English speaking nation. I thought that it would be very much easier for them to understand us, and for us to understand them, if they had a good working knowledge of the English language. While I appreciated the desirability of maintaining their grasp on the Spanish language, the beauty of that language, and the richness of its literature, that as a practical matter for them it was quite necessary to have a good comprehension of English."

May 20, 1927—*The Talkative President* p. 242

PUBLIC AFFAIRS

"Everybody must take a more active part in public affairs. It will not do for men to send, they must go. It is not enough to draw a check."

November 1, 1919—*Have Faith in Massachusetts* p. 271

PUBLIC OFFICE

"I do not feel that there is any more obligation to run for office than there is to become a banker, a merchant, a teacher, or enter any other special occupation. . . . Some men have a particular aptitude in this direction and some have none. Of course experience counts here as in any other human activity, and all experience worth the name is the result of application, of time and thought and study and practice. If the individual finds he has liking and capacity for this work, he will involuntarily find himself engaged in it. There is no catalogue of such a capacity."

President Coolidge (Whiting), p. xiv

PUBLIC PROPERTY

"We must have no carelessness in our dealings with public property or with the expenditure of public money. Such a condition is characteristic either of an undeveloped people or a decadent civilization."

Foundations of the Republic p. 46

PUBLIC SERVICE

"Public service, from the humblest voter to the most exalted office, can not be made a mere matter of hire and salary. The supporters of our institutions must be inspired by a more dominant motive than a conviction that their actions are going to be profitable. We can not lower our standards to what we think will pay, but we must raise them to what we think is right."

Foundations of the Republic pp. 26-27

"The government cannot be run successfully by substituting the power of entertainment for the power of accomplishment. The essential quality for the voters to require in their candidates is capacity for public service."

Calvin Coolidge Says October 8, 1930

RADICALISM

"It consisted of the claim in general that in some way the government was to be blamed because everybody was not prosperous, because it was necessary to work for a living, and because our written constitutions, the legislatures, and the courts protected the rights of private owners especially in relation to large aggregations of property."

Autobiography of Calvin Coolidge p. 107

RADIO

"I am very fortunate that I came in with the radio. I can't make an engaging, rousing, or oratorical speech to a crowd . . . , and so all I can do is stand up and talk to them in a matter-of-fact way about the issues of my campaign; but I have a good radio voice, and now I can get my messages across to them without acquainting them with my lack of oratorical ability or without making any rhetorical display in their presence."

To Senator James E. Watson, *Meet Calvin Coolidge* p. 144

REACTIONARIES

"Sometimes the person is not well thought of and he is labeled a reactionary. Sometimes if he is well thought of he is called a progressive."

July 18, 1924—*The Talkative President* p. 9

REGULATION

"The attempt to regulate, control, and prescribe all manner of conduct and social relations is very old. It was always the practice of primitive peoples."

August 10, 1922—*The Price of Freedom* p. 196

"There is no justification for public interference with purely private concerns."

August 10, 1922—*The Price of Freedom* p. 197

"We have had many attempts at regulation of industrial activity by law. Some of it has proceeded on the theory that if those who enjoyed material prosperity used it for wrong purposes, such prosperity should be limited or abolished. That is as sound as it would be to abolish writing to prevent forgery."

December 15, 1916—*Law and Order* pp. 30-31
Adequate Brevity p. 52

"You men who represent our industries can see that there is the same right to disperse unlawful assembling of wealth or power that there is to disperse a mob that has met to lynch or riot. But that principle does not denounce town-meetings or prayer-meetings."

December 15, 1916—*Law and Order* p. 31

"We have got so many regulatory laws already that in general I feel that we would be just as well off if we didn't have any more."

January 6, 1925—*The Talkative President* p. 123

"I am in favor of reducing, rather than expanding, Government bureaus which seek to regulate and control the business activities of the people. Everyone is aware that abuses exist and will exist so long as we are limited by human imperfections. Unfortunately, human nature can not be changed by an act of the legislature. When practically the sole remedy for many evils lies in the necessity of the people looking out for themselves and reforming their own abuses, they will find that they are relying on a false security if the Government assumes to hold out the promise that it is looking out for them and providing reforms for them. This principle is pre-eminently applicable to the National Government. It is too much assumed that because an abuse exists it is the business of the National Government to provide a remedy. The presumption should be that it is the business of local and state governments. Such national action results in encroaching upon the salutary independence of the States and by undertaking to supersede their natural authority fills the land with bureaus and departments, which are undertaking to do what it is impossible for them to accomplish and brings our whole system of government into disrespect and disfavor. We ought to maintain high standards. We ought to punish wrongdoing. Society has not only the privilege but the absolute duty of protecting itself and its individuals. But we can not accomplish this end by adopting a wrong method. Permanent success lies in local, rather than national action. Unless the locality rises to its own requirements, there is an almost irresistible impulse for the National Government to intervene. The States and the Nation should both realize that such action is to be adopted only as a last resort."

Fourth Annual Message to Congress, December 7, 1926
Messages and Papers of the Presidents pp. 9624-25

"It is always possible to regulate and supervise by legislation what has already been created, but while legislation can stimulate and encourage, the real creative ability which builds up and develops the country, and in general makes human existence more tolerable and life more complete, has to be supplied by the genius of the people themselves. The Government can supply no substitute for enterprise."

Foundations of the Republic p. 56

"We need a better cooperation between business and government. It would be well to temper regulation with co-operation and season restriction with encouragement."

Calvin Coolidge Says December 30, 1930

"Certain regulation is necessary, but a wise administration of regulatory laws increases greatly the employing power of the nation."

Calvin Coolidge Says December 19, 1930

RELIGION

"It was because religion gave the people a new importance and a new glory that they demanded a new freedom and a new government. We cannot in our generation reject the cause and retain the result."

April 13, 1923—*The Price of Freedom* p. 294
The Preparation of Calvin Coolidge p. 198
Adequate Brevity p. 87

"It is my own belief that in this land of freedom new arrivals should especially keep up their devotion to religion. Disregarding the need of the individual for a religious life, I feel that there is a more urgent necessity, based on the requirements of good citizenship and the maintenance of our institutions, for devotion to religion in America than anywhere else in the world. One of the greatest dangers that beset those coming to this country, especially those of the younger generation, is that they will fall away from the religion of their fathers, and never become attached to any other faith."

To immigrants, October 16, 1924
The Mind of the President p. 223

"Religion has laid the foundation of government."

January 21, 1923—*The Price of Freedom* p. 229

"We do not need more law, we need more religion. We do not need more of the things that are seen, we need more of the things that are unseen."

June 19, 1923—*The Price of Freedom* p. 390

"A spring will cease to flow if its source be dried up; a tree will wither if its roots be destroyed. In its main features the Declaration of Independence is a great spiritual document. It is a document not of material but of spiritual conceptions. Equality, liberty, popular sovereignty, the rights of men—these are not elements which we can see and touch. They are ideals. They have their source and roots in the religious convictions. They belong to the unseen world. Unless the faith of the American people in these religious convictions is to endure, the principles of the Declaration will perish. We can not continue to enjoy the result if we neglect and abandon the cause."

Third Annual Message to Congress, December 8, 1925

"If we wish to continue to be distinctively American, we must continue to make that term comprehensive enough to embrace the legitimate desires of a civilized and enlightened people determined in all their relations to pursue a conscientious and religious life."

Inaugural Address, March 5, 1925
Messages and Papers of the Presidents p. 9482

"Our government rests upon religion. It is from that source that we derive our reverence for truth and justice, for equality and liberty, and for the rights of mankind. Unless the people believe in these principles they cannot believe in our government. There are only two main theories of government in the world. One rests on righteousness, the other rests on force. One appeals to reason, the other appeals to the sword. One is exemplified in a republic, the other is represented by a despotism."

Speech honoring Bishop Francis Asbury, October 15, 1924

RELIGIOUS INSTRUCTION

"If attendance on these religious services ever harmed any of the men of my time I have never been informed of it."

Autobiography of Calvin Coolidge p . 55

REFORM

"Under a system of popular government there will always be those who will seek for political preferment by clamoring for reform. While there is very little of this which is not sincere, there is a large portion that is not well informed. In my opinion very little of just criticism can attach to the theories and principles of our institutions. There is far more danger of harm than there is hope of good in any radical changes."

Third Annual Message to Congress, December 8, 1925
Messages and Papers of the Presidents p. 9583

REPORTS

"When I begin to get reports on matters it usually means that there is some question for my decision. When I do not get reports it means everything is going all right."

August 14, 1928—*The Talkative President* p. 252

REPRESENTATIVE GOVERNMENT

"We need forever to remember that representative government does represent. A careless, indifferent representative is the result of a careless, indifferent electorate."

Have Faith in Massachusetts p. 79

REPUBLICAN PARTY

"The [Republican Party], through its present declaration of principles, through the traditions which it inherited from its predecessors, the Federalists and the Whigs, through their achievements and its own, is representative of those policies which were adopted under the lead of Alexander Hamilton. They are the parties which have kept steadily in view the Union and the whole Union. They cherished it through the necessary compromises of Henry Clay. They supported it through the wise and patient statesmanship of Abraham Lincoln. Without their vision the Union would never have been formed. Without their sacrifice it would not have been preserved."

January 11, 1922—*The Price of Freedom* p. 109

"It is the doctrine of the Republican Party to encourage business, not merely for its own sake but because that is the surest method of administering to the general welfare. Those who criticize will be justified in their criticism when they can point out a better way."

January 11, 1922—*The Price of Freedom* p. 112

"The Republican Party will in the future, as in the past, ever stand opposed to the establishment of one class who shall live on the government, and another class who shall pay the taxes."

Adequate Brevity p. 91

"The government under the Republican Party will continue in the future to be so administered as to breed not mendicants, but men."

Adequate Brevity p. 91

RETIREMENT FROM THE PRESIDENCY

"People seem to think the Presidential machinery should keep on running, even after the power has been turned off."

To author Bruce Barton, *Meet Calvin Coolidge* p. 191

REVERE, PAUL

"He became a hero only because the land was filled with heroism."

April 18, 1923—*The Price of Freedom* pp. 324-25

REVERENCE

"Reverence . . . is the beginning of a proper conception of ourselves, of our relationship to each other, and our relationship to our Creator. Human nature cannot develop very far without it. The mind does not unfold, the creative faculty does not mature, the spirit does not unfold, the creative faculty does not mature, the spirit does not expand, save under the influence of reverence. It is the chief motive of obedience. It is only by a correct attitude of mind begun early in youth and carried through maturity that these desired results are likely to be secured. It is along the path of reverence and obedience that the race has reached the goal of freedom, of self-government, of a higher morality, and a more abundant spiritual life."

Foundations of the Republic p. 104

REVOLUTION

"If a revolution meant a cleaning up of a bad situation and the substitution of a stable, permanent and free government it would have some merit. But when it means only a loss of life and property in order to substitute a new regime that is no better than the old, it accomplishes no constructive purpose. That is the reason our people regard revolutions with so much suspicion. They do not consider them as productive of genuine reform."

Calvin Coolidge Says August 25, 1930

RIGHT

"The right thing to do never requires any subterfuges, it is always simple and direct."

Autobiography of Calvin Coolidge, p. 135

RIGHTS

"The individual has rights, but only the citizen has the power to protect rights. And the protection of rights is righteous."

Adequate Brevity p. 19

"If ever the citizen comes to feel that our government does not protect him in the free and equal assertion of his rights at home and abroad, he will withdraw his allegiance from that government, as he ought to, and bestow it on some more worthy object."

Adequate Brevity p. 19

RUSSIA

"It comes down to this: Russia has a right to her Soviets or whatever she wants, so long as she doesn't disturb us. But to send a million dollars and a hundred agitators to China or to the United States is as much a making of war as would be the sending of an army."

To newspaperman Herman Beaty, *Meet Calvin Coolidge* p. 178

SACRIFICE

"We need wealth and science and justice in human relationship, but redemption comes only through sacrifice."

The Preparation of Calvin Coolidge p. 198

SAVINGS

"I know very well what it means to awake in the night and realize that the rent is coming due, wondering where the money is coming from with which to pay it. The only way I know of escape from that constant tragedy is to keep expenses low enough so that something may be saved to meet the day when earnings may be small."

Autobiography of Calvin Coolidge p. 94

SATISFACTION

"The society which is satisfied is lost."

August 10, 1922—*The Price of Freedom* p. 196

SCANDALS, HARDING

"If there has been any crime, it must be prosecuted. If there has been any property of the United States illegally transferred or leased, it must be recovered. . . . I propose to employ special counsel of high rank drawn from both political parties to bring such actions for the enforcement of the law. Counsel will be instructed to prosecute these cases in the courts so that if there is any guilt it will be punished; if there is any civil liability it will be enforced; if there is any fraud it will be revealed; and if there are any contracts which are illegal they will be canceled. Every law will be enforced. And every right of the people and the Government will be protected."

Quoted in *The New York Times*, January 27, 1924

SELF-GOVERNMENT

"Self-government means self support."

January 7, 1914—*Have Faith in Massachusetts* p. 5
Adequate Brevity p. 95

"The normal must care for themselves."

January 7, 1914—*Have Faith in Massachusetts* p. 5

"Self-government cannot be reposed wholly in some distant capital; it has to be exercised in part by the people in their own homes."

August 10, 1922—*The Price of Freedom* p. 198

"Our country was conceived in the theory of local self-government. It has been dedicated by long practice to that wise and beneficent policy. It is the foundation principle of our system of liberty. It makes the largest promise to the freedom and development of the individual. Its preservation is worth all the effort and all the sacrifice that it may cost.

"It cannot be denied that the present tendency is not in harmony with this spirit. The individual, instead of working out his own salvation and securing his own freedom by establishing his own economic and moral independence by his own industry and his own self-mastery, tends to throw himself on some vague influence which he denominates society and to hold that in some way responsible for the sufficiency of his support and the morality of his actions. The local political units likewise look to the States, the States look to the Nation, and nations are beginning to look to some vague organization, some nebulous concourse of humanity, to pay their bills and tell them what to do. This is not local self-government. It is not America. It is not the method which has made this country what it is. We cannot maintain the western standard of civilization on that theory. If it is supported at all, it will have to be supported on the principle of individual responsibility."

Address at Arlington National Cemetery, May 30, 1925
The Mind of the President pp. 70-71

"We demand entire freedom of action and then expect the government in some miraculous way to save us from the consequences of our own acts. We want the right to run our own business, fix our own wages and prices, and spend our own money, but if depression and unemployment result we look to government for a remedy.

"We insist on producing a farm surplus, but think the government should find a profitable market for it. We overindulge in speculation, but ask the government to prevent panics. Now the only way to hold the government entirely responsible for conditions is to give up our liberty for a dictatorship. If we continue the more reasonable practice of managing our own affairs we must bear the burdens of our own mistakes. A free people cannot shift their responsibility for them to the government. Self-government means self-reliance."

Calvin Coolidge Says October 17, 1930

SELF-SUPPORT

"I have no respect for anybody who cannot take care of himself."

Calvin Coolidge: Man From Vermont p. 193

SELFISHNESS

"Selfishness is only another name for suicide."

Adequate Brevity p. 96

SENATE, UNITED STATES

". . . I soon found that the Senate had but one fixed rule, subject to exceptions of course, which was to the effect that the Senate would do anything it wanted to do whenever it wanted to do it. When I had learned that, I did not waste much time with the other rules, because they were so seldom applied."

Autobiography of Calvin Coolidge p. 162

"If the Senate has any weakness it is because the people have sent to that body men lacking the necessary ability and character to perform the proper functions. But that is not the fault of the Senate. It cannot choose its own members but has to work with what is sent to it."

Autobiography of Calvin Coolidge p. 163

SERVICE

"No person was ever honored for what he received. Honor has been the reward for what he gave."

Veto of Salary Increase—*Have Faith in Massachusetts* p. 173

"The possession of property carries the obligation to use it in a larger service."

Autobiography of Calvin Coolidge p. 67

"The principle of service is not to be confused with a weak and impractical sentimentalism."

Adequate Brevity p. 98

"Public acclaim and the ceremonious recognition paid to returning heroes are not on account of their government pay but of the service and sacrifice they gave their country."

Adequate Brevity p. 100

SPENDING

"I know how to save money. All my training has been in that direction. The country is in a sound financial condition. Perhaps the time has come when we ought to spend money. I do not feel I am qualified to do that."

Ishbel Ross, *Grace Coolidge*, p. 226

SHYNESS

"When I was a little fellow, as long as I can remember, I would go into a panic if I heard strange voices in the house. I felt I just couldn't meet people, and shake hands with them. Most of the visitors would sit with Mother and Father in the kitchen, and it was the hardest thing in the world to have to go through the kitchen door and give them a greeting. I was almost ten before I realized I couldn't go on that way. And by fighting hard I used to manage to get through that door. I'm all right with old friends, but every time I meet a stranger, I've got to go through the old kitchen door, back home, and it's not easy."

Coolidge: An American Enigma, p. 25

SLEEP

"In Washington I went to sleep pretty quickly, but if I had a hard problem on my mind, I would wake up in the middle of the night, and the tougher the problem, the earlier I waked up. Sometimes it was hard to go to sleep again. Of course, everything a President does is subjected to criticism. But I used to remind myself that the criticism probably wouldn't bulk very large in the pages of history, and then I would reflect that the country seemed to be in pretty sound condition. So I would roll over and go to sleep."

To author Bruce Barton, *Meet Calvin Coolidge* pp. 190-91

SOCIAL DINNERS

"As we were always the ranking guests we had the privilege of arriving last and leaving first, so that we were usually home by ten o'clock. It will be seen that this was far from burdensome."

Autobiography of Calvin Coolidge p. 160

SPEAKING

"My fellow countrymen have put me in situations where I have found I could not refrain from speaking."

To the Gridiron Club Dinner, December 1923, *Meet Calvin Coolidge* p. 9

"I don't recall any candidate for President that ever injured himself very much by not talking."

September 16, 1924—*The Talkative President* p. 10

SPENDING

"Nothing is easier than spending the public money. It does not appear to belong to anybody. The temptation is overwhelming to bestow it on somebody."

Quoted in *Readers Digest*, June 1960, p. 178

"The appropriation of public money always is perfectly lovely until some one is asked to pay the bill. If we are to have a billion dollars of navy, half a billion of farm relief, [etc.] . . . the people will have to furnish more revenue by paying more taxes. It is for them, through their Congress, to decide how far they wish to go."

Syndicated column, *New York Herald Tribune*, August 5, 1930, p. 1

"I would not want to be misunderstood. I am not advocating parsimony. I want to be liberal. Public service is entitled to a suitable reward. But there is a distinct limit to the amount of public service we can profitably employ. We require national defense, but it must be limited. We need public improvements, but they must be gradual. We have to make capital investments, but they must be certain to give fair returns. Every dollar expended must be made in the light of all our national resources and all our national needs."

At Memorial Continental Hall, June 30, 1924
The Mind of the President p. 114

SPORTS

"There is a place, both present and future, for true, clean sport. We do not rank it above business, the occupations of our lives, and we do not look with approval upon those who, not being concerned in its performance, spend all their thought, energy and time upon its observance. We recognize, however, that there is something more in life than the grinding routine of daily toil, that we can develop a better manhood and womanhood, a more mature youth and a wiser maturity by rounding out our existence with a wholesome interest in sport.

"To those who devote themselves to this enterprise in a professional way and, by throwing their whole being into it, raise it to the level of an art, the country owes a debt of gratitude. They furnish us with amusement, with an outside interest, oftentimes, in the open air that quickens the step, refreshes the mind, rejuvenates and restores us."

Washington, D.C., October 12, 1924

"All of the varied sports activities take people out of doors where they relax, recuperate and gain new interests that broaden and sweeten life. They afford an outlet for primitive instincts which otherwise tend to turn in upon themselves, with disaster to the normal development of the individual and at cost to society. Plenty of playgrounds and games is the best cure for youthful delinquency. Plenty of outdoor sports is a wise investment in good citizenship."

Calvin Coolidge Says September 12, 1930

STATES RIGHTS

"The doctrine of State rights is not a privilege to continue in wrong-doing but a privilege to be free from interference in well-doing."

Coolidge and the Historians p. 27

"We cannot improve the condition of the people or reform human nature by intruding the nation into the affairs of the states or despoiling the people of their business."

Calvin Coolidge Says June 26, 1931

STRIKES

"There is no right to strike against the public safety by anybody, anywhere, any time."

To Samuel Gompers, September 14, 1919
Have Faith in Massachusetts p. 223

SUCCESS

"The measure of success is not merchandise but character."

February 4, 1916—*Have Faith in Massachusetts* p. 14

"I do not think that men who look at every little part of the whole can ever be very successful. The day laborers never do any work quite so disagreeable or dirty as does the chemist or the physician yet the one is degraded and the other ennobled simply because one sees the relation and views the part in the light of the whole and is a head while the other sees only the part and is a hand."

May 13, 1895—*Your Son Calvin Coolidge* p. 69

"Success comes to people who are not considering the narrow question of what they are paid for, but the broad question of what they can do to be helpful. It is that attitude which leads to the promotion of the individual, the profit of the business and the prosperity of the nation."

Calvin Coolidge Says August 1, 1930

SURVIVAL OF THE FITTEST

"The law of progress and civilization is not the law of the jungle. It is not an earthly law, it is a divine law. It does not mean survival of the fittest, it means sacrifice of the fittest. Any mother will give her life for her child. Men put women and children in lifeboats before they themselves will leave the sinking ship. John Hampden and Nathan Hale did not survive, nor did Lincoln, but Benedict Arnold did."

June 17, 1918—*Have Faith in Massachusetts* p. 118

TAXES

"As I went about with my father when he collected taxes, I knew that when taxes were laid some one had to work to earn money to pay them."

Autobiography of Calvin Coolidge p. 26

"The property of the people belongs to the people. To take it from them by taxation cannot be justified except by urgent public necessity. Unless this principle be recognized our country is no longer secure, our people no longer free."

Adequate Brevity p. 108

"The first object of taxation is to secure revenue."

Coolidge and the Historians (Silver) p. 109

" . . . if the rates of large incomes are so high that they disappear, the small taxpayer will be left to bear the entire burden. If on the other hand, the rates are placed where they will secure the most revenue from large incomes, then the small taxpayer will be relieved."

Coolidge and the Historians (Silver) p. 109

"The business of the country, as a whole, is transacted on a small margin of profit. The economic structure is one of great delicacy and sensitiveness. When taxes become too burdensome, either the price of commodities has to be raised to a point at which consumption is so diminished as greatly to curtail production, or so much of the returns from industry is required by the government that production becomes unprofitable and ceases for that reason. In either case there is depression, lack of employment, idleness of investment and of the wage-earner, with the long line of attendant want and suffering on the part of the people. After order and liberty, economy is one of the highest essentials of a free government."

May 30, 1923—The Price of Freedom p. 350

"A government which requires of the people the contribution of the bulk of their substance and rewards cannot be classed as a free government, or long remain as such."

May 30, 1923—The Price of Freedom p. 351

"The collection of any taxes which are not absolutely required, which do not beyond reasonable doubt contribute to the public welfare, is only a species of legalized larceny. Under this republic the rewards of industry belong to those who earn them. The only constitutional tax is the tax which ministers to public necessity. The property of the country belongs to the people of the country. Their title is absolute. They do not support any privileged class; they do not need to maintain great military forces; they ought not to be burdened with a great array of public employees."

Inaugural Address, March 4, 1925
The Mind of the President pp. 108-09
Messages and Papers of the Presidents p. 9486

"The method of raising revenue ought not to impede the transaction of business; it ought to encourage it. I am opposed to extremely high rates, because they produce little or no revenue, because they are bad for the country, and, finally, because they are wrong. We can not finance the country, we can not improve social conditions, through any system of injustice, even if we attempt to inflict it upon the rich. Those who suffer the most harm will be the poor. This country believes in prosperity. It is absurd to suppose that it is envious of those who are already prosperous. The wise and correct course to follow in taxation and all other economic legislation is not to destroy those who have already secured success but to create conditions under which every one will have a better chance to be successful. The verdict of the country has been given on this question. That verdict stands. We shall do well to heed it."

Inaugural Address, March 4, 1925
The Mind of the President pp. 125-26

"I want the people of America to be able to work less for the Government and more for themselves. I want them to have the rewards of their own industry. That is the chief meaning of freedom."

Inaugural Address, March 4, 1925
The Mind of the President p. 111

"There is a limit to the taxing power of a State beyond which increased rates produce decreased revenues. If that be exceeded intangible securities and other personal property become driven out of its jurisdiction, industry cannot meet its less burdened competitors, and no capital will be found for enlarging old or starting new enterprises. Such a condition means first stagnation, then decay and dissolution."

January 8, 1920—*Law and Order* p. 47

"That tax is theoretically best which interferes least with business. Every student knows that excessively high tax rates defeat their own purpose.

They dry up that source of revenue and leave those paying lower rates to furnish all the taxes."

Calvin Coolidge of Northampton pp. 12-13

"A government which lays taxes on the people not required by urgent public necessity and sound public policy is not a protector of liberty, but an instrument of tyranny. It condemns the citizen to servitude. One of the first signs of the breaking down of a free government is a disregard by the taxing power of the right of the people to their own property. It makes little difference whether such a condition is brought about through will of a dictator, through the power of a military force, or through the pressure of an organized minority. The result is the same. Unless the people can enjoy that reasonable security in the possession of their property, which is guaranteed in the Constitution, against unreasonable taxation, freedom is at an end. The common man is restrained and hampered in his ability to secure food and clothing and shelter. His wages are decreased, his hours are lengthened. Against the recurring tendency in this direction there must be interposed the constant effort of an informed electorate and of patriotic public servants. The importance of a constant reiteration of these principles cannot be overestimated."

At Memorial Continental Hall, June 30, 1924
The Mind of the President p. 113
Foundations of the Republic pp. 40-41

"High taxes make high prices."

January 8, 1920—*Law and Order* p. 48

"Taxes must be paid by the public. They cannot be imposed on any class. There is no power that can prevent a distribution of the burden. The landlord may be the one who sends a check to the public treasury, but his tenants nevertheless make the payment. A great manufacturer may contribute a large share to his income, but still the money comes from the consumer. Taxes must and do fall on the people in whatever form or name they are laid."

January 8, 1920—*Law and Order* p. 48

"I can lay down the broad principle that I am not in favor of imposing any new kinds of taxes."

April 2, 1924—The Mind of the President p. 117

"No matter what any one may say about making the rich and the corporations pay the taxes, in the end they come out of the people who toil. It is your fellow workers who are ordered to work for the Government every time an appropriation bill is passed."

To labor leaders, September 1, 1924
The Mind of the President p. 125

"One of the rights which the freeman has always guarded with the jealous care is that of enjoying the rewards of his own industry. Realizing the power to tax is the power to destroy, and that the power to take a certain amount of property or of income is only another way of saying that for a certain amount of his time a citizen must work for the government, the authority to impose a tax upon the people must be carefully guarded. . . . It condemns the citizen to servitude."

Coolidge: An American Enigma p. 312

"Whenever the state of the Treasury can permit, I believe in a reduction of taxes. But I am not advocating tax reduction merely for the benefit of the taxpayer; I am advocating it for the benefit of the country."

Fourth Annual Message to Congress, December 7, 1926
Messages and Papers of the Presidents p. 9614

"There is no escaping the fact that when the taxation of large incomes is excessive, they tend to disappear."

Adequate Brevity p. 105

"The success of the Government does not lie in wringing all the revenue it can from the people, but in making their burden as light and fairly distributed as possible, consistent with the proper maintenance of the necessary public functions."

Adequate Brevity p. 108

"I want taxes to be less, that the people may have more."

September 1, 1924

The Mind of the President p. 105

TAX-FREE BONDS

"Another reform which is urgent in our fiscal system is the abolition of the right to issue tax-exempt securities. The existing system not only permits a large amount of the wealth of the nation to escape its just burden, but acts as a continual stimulant to municipal extravagance. This should be prohibited by constitutional amendment. All the wealth of the nation ought to contribute its fair share to the expenses of the nation."

Annual Message to Congress, December 6, 1923

The Mind of the President p. 113

"A man with large inherited or accumulated capital is told he must pay one half of his income to the Government if he invests in productive business, but he is invited to be relieved of all tax by the simple expedient of withdrawing from business and investing in tax-exempt securities. That does not mean that wealth in existence is taxed; it is not. It escapes. It does mean, however, that initiative and new enterprises are throttled."

Statement, June 2, 1924

The Mind of the President p. 119

TAX RATES

"If we had a tax whereby on the first working day the Government took 5 per cent of your wages, on the second day 10 per cent, on the third day 20 per cent, on the fourth day 30 per cent, on the fifth day 50 per cent, and on the sixth day 60 per cent, how many of you would continue to work on the last two days of the week? It is the same with capital. Surplus income will go into tax-exempt securities. It will refuse to take the risk incidental to embarking in business. This will raise the rate which established business will have to pay for new capital, and result in a marked increase in the cost of living. If new capital will not flow into competing enterprise, the present concerns tend toward monopoly, increasing again the prices which the people must pay."

To the National Republican Club, February 12, 1924

The Mind of the President p. 129

TEACHERS

"There no doubt often arises a feeling on the part of the teaching force of the nation that they are lacking in public appreciation. They do not occupy positions which bring them into general prominence. Their compensation is not large in any event and considering the length of time and the necessary expense required in preparation is often very meager. But if their rewards are not large, they are seldom exposed to that species of criticism, often turning into positive abuse, which is the lot of many elected public servants."

December 21, 1922—*The Price of Freedom* pp. 211-12

THANKSGIVING

"If at any time our rewards have seemed meager, we should find our justification for Thanksgiving by carefully comparing what we have with what we deserve."

Calvin Coolidge Says November 27, 1930

TOIL

"Government cannot relieve from toil."

January 7, 1914—*Have Faith in Massachusetts* p. 5

TOURISTS

"Two kinds of tourists go abroad. One kind are of a somewhat bumptious nature. If that kind of tourist gets some education abroad and finds out there are other people in the world that are entitled to some consideration and respect them as well as Americans, I don't think that will do any great harm. There is another kind of people that go abroad that have an appreciation of the amenities that are usually practiced, and if they do not find things to their liking abroad of course their remedy is to come home and stay here and spend their money here."

July 27, 1926—*The Talkative President* p. 210

"While our tourists will find many things to admire and some to emulate, a careful investigation will convince them that the general condition of the people of their own country is unsurpassed. They will return for the most part more content with their own institutions, more loyal to their own government, more devoted to their own faith. Those who do not will not be of great consequence."

Calvin Coolidge Says July 5, 1930

TROUBLE

"Never go out of your way to meet trouble. If you will just sit still, nine cases out of ten, someone will intercept it before it reaches you."

Era of Excess (Sinclair) p. 252

"Don't you know four-fifths of all our troubles in this life would disappear if we would only sit down and keep still?"

To Senator James Watson

TRUTH

"While the quantity of the truth we know may be small it is the quality that is important. If we really knew the truth the quality of our knowledge could not be surpassed by the Infinite."

Autobiography of Calvin Coolidge p. 65

VERMONT

"Vermont is a state I love.

"I could not look upon the peaks of Ascutney, Killington, Mansfield and Equinox without being moved in a way that no other scene could move me.

"It was here that I first saw the light of day; here I received my bride; here my dead lie pillowed on the loving breast of our everlasting hills.

"I love Vermont because of her hills and valleys, her scenery and invigorating climate, but most of all, because of her indomitable people. They are a race of pioneers who have almost beggared themselves to serve others. If the spirit of liberty should vanish in other parts of the union and support of our institutions should languish, it could all be replenished from the generous store held by the people of this brave little state of Vermont."

September 21, 1928, Bennington, Vermont

"Vermont is my birthright. Here one gets close to nature, in the mountains, in the brooks, the waters which hurry to the sea; in the lakes, shining like silver in their green setting; fields tilled, not by machinery, but by the brain and hand of man. My folks are happy and contented. They belong to themselves, live within their incomes, and fear no man."

Calvin Coolidge: Man From Vermont p. 11

VETERANS

"A country worth defending takes care of its defenders."

October 31, 1921—*The Price of Freedom* p. 89

VICE-PRESIDENCY

"It was my intention when I became Vice-President to remain in Washington, avoid speaking and to attend to the work of my office. But the pressure to speak is constant and intolerable. However, I resisted most of it."

Autobiography of Calvin Coolidge p. 164

VISITORS

"You have to stand every day three or four hours of visitors. Nine-tenths of them want something they ought not to have. If you keep dead-still they will run down in three or four minutes. If you even cough or smile they will start up all over again."

The Real Calvin Coolidge p. 59

VOTING

"A considerable part of those who neglect to vote do it because of a curious assumption of superiority to this elementary duty of the citizen. They presume to be rather too good, too exclusive, to soil their hands with the work of politics. Such an attitude cannot too vigorously be condemned."

The Mind of the President p. 93

WAGES

"The greater the profit, the greater the wages."

September 1, 1919—*Have Faith in Massachusetts* p. 202

"Those who do only what they are paid for will never be paid very much."

Calvin Coolidge Says August 1, 1930

WALKER, MAYOR JAMES J.

"He has the Celtic ability to put all his goods in front window—and leave none in reserve; he has shrewdness rather than any real ability; the kind of man who, if you wake him from a sound sleep to make a speech, is able to start right in speaking. But if you examine the speech later, you will find he has said nothing worth while."

To newspaperman Herman Beaty, *Meet Calvin Coolidge*, p. 177

WAR

"The only hope of a short war is to prepare for a long one."

August 7, 1918—*Have Faith in Massachusetts* p. 129

WASHINGTON

"It is necessary to watch people in Washington all the time to keep them from unnecessary expenditure of money. They have all lived off the national Government so long in that city that they are inclined to regard any sort of employment as a Christmas tree, and if we are not careful, they will run up a big expense bill on us."

The Real Calvin Coolidge p. 136

WASHINGTON SENATORS

"As the head of an enterprise which transacts some business and maintains a considerable staff in this town, I have a double satisfaction in welcoming home the victorious Washington baseball team. First, you bring the laurels from one of the hardest-fought contests in the history of the national game. Second, I feel hopeful that, with the happy result now assured, it will be possible for the people of Washington gradually to resume interest in the ordinary concerns of life.

"So long as we could be satisfied with a prompt report of the score by innings a reasonable attention to business was still possible. But when the entire population reached the point of requiring the game to be described play by play, I began to doubt whether the highest efficiency was being promoted. I contemplated action of a vigorously disciplinary character, but the outcome makes it impossible. As a result, we are a somewhat demoralized community—but exceedingly happy over it."

Welcoming the Washington Senators,
1924 American League pennant winners, October 11, 1924

WEALTH

"Accumulated wealth will be of very little value to society unless it voluntarily comes to the rescue in time to prevent public suffering."

Calvin Coolidge Says October 10, 1930

WEALTH, DISTRIBUTION OF

"Our country is an exceedingly good example of the fact that if production be encouraged and increased, then distribution fairly well takes care of itself. Other countries, by their actions in stopping production, in penalizing industry and economy, and rewarding indolence and extravagance, have been able to bring about a very general and equal distribution of misery, but no other country ever approached ours in the equal and general distribution of prosperity."

June 19, 1923—*The Price of Freedom* p. 389

WHITTLING

"I mentioned the other day that any reports about what I was going to do when I finished being President were made entirely without consultation by me. I forgot to mention one report that is going around. I mention it now because I don't want to be accused of acquiring property under false pretenses. I am having sent to me quite a number of jackknives. I don't recall that I ever made any suggestion that after I finished my term of office I was going to engage in the occupation of whittling. I did some when I was a boy. I haven't applied myself to that for a good many years. I hesitate to spoil anything like a good newspaper story, but as I say, I don't want to keep getting jackknives under false pretenses."

January 3, 1928—*The Talkative President* p. 16

WOMEN

"What men owe to the love and help of good women can never be told."

Autobiography of Calvin Coolidge p. 44

"Men build monuments above the graves of their heroes to mark the end of a great life, but women seek out the birthplace and build their shrine, not where a great life had its ending but where it had its beginning, seeking with a truer instinct the common source of things not in that which is gone forever but in that which they know will again be manifest."

January 23, 1921—*The Price of Freedom* p. 18

"A woman is essentially a conservative. She wants to assure to the last degree protection for her children."

To newspaperman Herman Beaty, *Meet Calvin Coolidge* p. 178

WORK

"Work is not a curse, it is a prerogative of intelligence, the only means to manhood, and the measure of civilization. Savages do not work. The growth of a sentiment that despises work is an appeal from civilization to barbarism."

June 17, 1918—*Have Faith in Massachusetts* p. 120

"One of the earliest mandates laid on the human race was to subdue the earth. That meant work."

Autobiography of Calvin Coolidge p. 68

"The growth of a sentiment that despises work is an appeal from civilization to barbarism."

February 4, 1916—*Have Faith in Massachusetts* p. 13

"I don't work at night. If a man can't finish his job in the day time he's not smart."

To Edmund W. Starling, *Meet Calvin Coolidge* p. 77

"America recognizes no aristocracy save those who work. The badge of service is the sole requirement for admission to the ranks of our nobility."

Foundations of the Republic p. 76

"It is not dissatisfaction with our work but dissatisfaction with ourselves that is the cause of the unrest and discomfort which is always manifesting itself in one form or another. We think we want to change our employment, when we really want to change ourselves."

Autobiography of Calvin Coolidge p. 387

"I cannot think of anything that represents the American people as a whole so adequately as honest work. We perform different tasks, but the spirit is the same. We are proud of work and ashamed of idleness. With us there is no task which is menial, no service which is degrading. All work is ennobling and all workers are ennobled."

Foundations of the Republic p. 75

"One of the great mysteries in the world is the success that lies in conscientious work."

Autobiography of Calvin Coolidge p. 100

WORSHIP

"Men show by what they worship what they are."

January 30, 1919—*Have Faith in Massachusetts* p. 167

"It is only when men begin to worship that they begin to grow."

July 6, 1922—*The Price of Freedom* p. 173

WRITING

"I am not conscious of having any particular style about my writings. If I have any, it is undoubtedly due to my training in the construction of legal papers, where it is necessary in the framing of a contract, or the drawing of a pleading, to say what you mean and mean what you say in terms sufficiently clear and concise so that your adversary will not be able to misinterpret them, or to divert the trial into a discussion of unimportant matters. The rule is to state the case with as little diffusion as possible."

Letter to Charles Willis Thompson, December 29, 1924
Calvin Coolidge: Man From Vermont p. 295

XENOPHOBIA

"Human nature provides sufficient distrust of all that is alien, so that there is no need of any artificial supply."

Before United Press, New York City, April 25, 1927
Messages and Papers of the Presidents p. 9691

(courtesy of the Library of Congress)

Selected Addresses of Calvin Coolidge

◆ ◆ ◆

"Have Faith in Massachusetts"

Calvin Coolidge's Address to the State Senate on being elected its President
Boston, Massachusetts, January 7, 1914

Honorable Senators:—I thank you—with gratitude for the high honor given, with appreciation for the solemn obligations assumed—I thank you.

This Commonwealth is one. We are all members of one body. The welfare of the weakest and the welfare of the most powerful are inseparably bound together. Industry cannot flourish if labor languish. Transportation cannot prosper if manufactures decline. The general welfare cannot be provided for in any one act, but it is well to remember that the benefit of one is the benefit of all, and the neglect of one is the neglect of all. The suspension of one man's dividends is the suspension of another man's pay envelope.

Men do not make laws. They do but discover them. Laws must be justified by something more than the will of the majority. They must rest on the eternal foundation of righteousness. That state is most fortunate in its form of government which has the aptest instruments for the discovery of laws. The latest, most modern, and nearest perfect system that statesmanship has devised is representative government. Its weakness is the weakness of us imperfect human beings who administer it. Its strength is that even such administration secures to the people more blessings than any other system ever produced. No nation has discarded it and retained liberty. Representative government must be preserved.

Courts are established, not to determine the popularity of a cause, but to adjudicate and enforce rights. No litigant should be required to submit his case to the hazard and expense of a political campaign. No judge should be required to seek or receive political rewards. The courts of Massachusetts are known and honored wherever men love justice.

Let their glory suffer no diminution at our hands. The electorate and judiciary cannot combine. A hearing means a hearing. When the trial of causes goes outside the court-room, Anglo-Saxon constitutional government ends.

The people cannot look to legislation generally for success. Industry, thrift, character, are not conferred by act or resolve. Government cannot relieve from toil. It can provide no substitute for the rewards of service. It can, of course, care for the defective and recognize distinguished merit. The normal must care for themselves. Self-government means self-support.

Man is born into the universe with a personality that is his own. He has a right that is founded upon the constitution of the universe to have property that is his own. Ultimately, property rights and personal rights are the same thing. The one cannot be preserved if the other be violated. Each man is entitled to his rights and the rewards of his service be they never so large or never so small.

History reveals no civilized people among whom there were not a highly educated class, and large aggregations of wealth, represented usually by the clergy and the nobility. Inspiration has always come from above.

Diffusion of learning has come down from the university to the common school—the kindergarten is last. No one would now expect to aid the common school by abolishing higher education.

It may be that the diffusion of wealth works in an analogous way. As the little red schoolhouse is builded in the college, it may be that the fostering and protection of large aggregations of wealth are the only foundation on which to build the prosperity of the whole people. Large profits mean large pay rolls. But profits must be the result of service performed. In no land are there so many and such large aggregations of wealth as here; in no land do they perform larger service; in no land will the work of a day bring so large a reward in material and spiritual welfare.

Have faith in Massachusetts. In some unimportant detail some other States may surpass her, but in the general results, there is no place on earth where the people secure, in a larger measure, the blessings of organized government, and nowhere can those functions more properly be termed self-government.

Do the day's work. If it be to protect the rights of the weak, whoever objects, do it. If it be to help a powerful corporation better to serve the people, whatever the opposition, do that. Expect to be called a stand-patter, but don't be a stand-patter. Expect to be called a demagogue, but don't be a demagogue. Don't hesitate to be as revolutionary as science. Don't hesitate to be as reactionary as the multiplication table. Don't expect to build up the weak by pulling down the strong. Don't hurry to legislate. Give administration a chance to catch up with legislation.

We need a broader, firmer, deeper faith in the people—a faith that men desire to do right, that the Commonwealth is founded upon a righteousness which will endure, a reconstructed faith that the final approval of the people is given not to demagogues, slavishly pandering to their selfishness, merchandising with the clamor of the hour, but to statesmen, ministering to their welfare, representing their deep, silent, abiding convictions.

Statutes must appeal to more than material welfare. Wages won't satisfy, be they never so large. Nor houses; nor lands; nor coupons, though they fall thick as the leaves of autumn. Man has a spiritual nature. Touch it, and it must respond as the magnet responds to the pole. To that, not to selfishness, let the laws of the Commonwealth appeal. Recognize the immortal worth and dignity of man. Let the laws of Massachusetts proclaim to her humblest citizen, performing the most menial task, the recognition of his manhood, the recognition that all men are peers, the humblest with the most exalted, the recognition that all work is glorified. Such is the path to equality before the law. Such is the foundation of liberty under the law. Such is the sublime revelation of man's relation to man—Democracy.

"Law and Order"
Calvin Coolidge's Second Inaugural Address as Governor of Massachusetts
January 8, 1920

It is preeminently the province of government to protect the weak. The average citizen does not lead the life of independence that was his in former days under a less complex order of society. When a family tilled the soil and produced its own support it was independent. It may be infinitely better off now, but it is evident it needs a protection which before was not required.

Let Massachusetts continue to regard with the greatest solicitude the well-being of her people. By prescribed law, by authorized publicity, by informed public opinion, let her continue to strive to provide that all conditions under which her citizens live are worthy of the highest faith of man. Healthful housing, wholesome food, sanitary working conditions, reasonable hours, a fair wage for a fair day's work, opportunity—full and free, justice—speedy and impartial, and at a cost within the reach of all, are among the objects not only to be sought, but made absolutely certain and secure.

Government is not, must not be, a cold, impersonal machine, but a human and more humane agency: appealing to the reason, satisfying the heart, full of mercy, assisting the good, resisting the wrong, delivering the weak from any impositions of the powerful. This is not paternalism. It is not a servitude imposed from without, but the freedom of a right to self-direction from within.

Industry must be humanized, not destroyed. It must be the instrument not of selfishness, but of service. Change not the law, but the attitude of the mind. Let our citizens look not to the false prophet but to the pilgrims. Let them fix their eyes on Plymouth Rock as well as Beacon Hill. The supreme choice must be not to things that are seen, but to things that are unseen.

Our government belongs to the people. Our property belongs to the people. It is distributed. They own it. The taxes are paid by the people. They bear the burden. The benefits of government must accrue to the people. Not to one class, but to all classes, to all the people. The functions, the power, the sovereignty of the government, must be kept where they have been placed by the Constitution and laws of the people. Not private will, but that public will, which speaks with a divine sanction, must prevail.

There are strident voices, urging resistance to law in the name of freedom. They are not seeking freedom for themselves, they have it. They are seeking to enslave others. Their works are evil. They know it. They must be resisted. The evil they represent must be overcome by the good others represent. Their ideas, which are wrong, for the most part imported, must be supplanted by ideas which are right. This can be done. The meaning of America is a power which cannot be overcome. Massachusetts must lead in teaching it.

Prosecution of the criminal and education of the ignorant are the remedies. It is fundamental that freedom is not to be secured by disobedience to law. Even the freedom of the slave depended on the supremacy of the Constitution. There is no mystery about this. They who sin are the servants of sin. They who break the laws are the slaves of their own kind. It is not for the advantage of others that the citizen is abjured to obey the laws, but for his own advantage. That what he claims a right to do to others, that must he admit others have a right to do to him. His obedience is his own protection. He is not submitting himself to the dictates of others, but responding to the requirements of his own nature.

Laws are not manufactured. They are not imposed. They are rules of action existing from everlasting to everlasting. He who resists them, resists himself. He commits suicide. The nature of man requires sovereignty. Government must govern. To obey is life. To disobey is death. Organized government is the expression of the life of the commonwealth. Into your hands is entrusted the grave responsibility of its protection and perpetuation.

Calvin Coolidge's Formal Acceptance of the Republican Vice-Presidential Nomination Northampton Massachusetts July 27, 1920

Governor [Edwin P.] Morrow [of Kentucky] and Members of the Notification Committee: To your now formal notification I respond with formal acceptance.

Your presence tells me of a leader and a cause; a leader in Warren G. Harding, the united choice of a united party, a statesman of ability, seasoned by experience, a fitting representative of the common aspirations of his fellow citizens, wise enough to seek counsel, great enough to recognize merit, and in all things a stalwart American; the cause of our common country, as declared in the platform of the Republican Party, the defense of our institutions from every assault, the restoration of constitutional government, the maintenance of law and order, the relief of economic distress, the encouragement of industry and agriculture, the enactment of humanitarian laws, the defense of the rights of our citizens everywhere, the rehabilitation of this nation in the estimation of all peoples, under an agreement, meeting our every duty, to preserve the peace of the world, always with unyielding Americanism under such a leader, such a cause, I serve.

No one in public life can be oblivious to the organized efforts to undermine the faith of our people in their government, foment, discord, aggravate industrial strife, stifle production, and ultimately stir up revolution. These efforts are a great public menace, not through danger of success, but through the great amount of harm they can do if ignored.

The first duty of the government is to repress them, punishing willful violations of law, turning the full light of publicity on all abuses of the right of assembly and of free speech; and it is the first duty of the public and press to expose false doctrines and answer seditious arguments.

American institutions can stand discussion and criticism, only if those who know bear for them the testimony of the truth. Such repression and such testimony should be forthcoming, that the uninformed may come to a full realization that these seditious efforts are not for their welfare, but for their complete economic and political destruction.

To a free people the most reactionary experience, short of revolution, is war. In order to organize and conduct military operations a reversion to an autocratic method of government is absolutely necessary. In our own case it was no less autocratic because voluntarily established by the people. It was a wise and successful process for the purpose of winning the victory of freedom, to which all else was a secondary consideration. But voluntary autocracy was established temporarily that freedom might be established permanently. Men submitted their persons and their property to the complete dictation of the government that they might conquer an impending peril.

This has always been fraught with the gravest dangers. It is along this path that rides the man on horseback. Avarice for power finds many reasons for continuing arbitrary action after the cause for which it was granted has been removed.

The government of the United States was not established for the continued prosecution, or the perpetual preparation, of all its resources for war. It has been and intends to be a nation devoted to the arts of peace. Fundamentally considered, its abiding purpose has been the recognition of the rights and the development of the individual. This great purpose has been accomplished through self-government. To the individual has been left power and responsibility, the foundation for the rule of the people. In time of emergency these are surrendered to the government in return for providing the necessaries of life, and national safety. But these are and must be temporary expedients, if we are to keep our form of government, and maintain the supreme purpose of Americans.

The greatest need of the nation at the present time is to be rescued from all the reactions of the war. The chief task that lies before us is to repossess the people of their government and their property. We want to return to a thoroughly peace basis because that is the fundamental American basis. Unless the government and property of the nation are in the hands of the people, and there to stay as their permanent abiding place, self-government ends and the hope of America goes down in ruins.

This need is transcendent.

The government of the nation is in the hands of the people, when it is administered in accordance with the spirit of the Constitution, which they have adopted and ratified, and which measures the powers they have granted to their public officers, in all its branches, where the functions and duties of the three co-ordinate branches, executive, legislative, judicial, are separate and distinct and neither one directly or indirectly exercises any of the functions of either of the others. Such a practice and such a government under the Constitution of the United States it is the purpose of our party to re-establish and maintain. All authority must be exercised by those to whom it is constitutionally entrusted, without dictation, and with responsibility only to those who have bestowed it, the people.

The property of the nation is in the hands of the people when it is under their ownership and control. It is true that the control of a part of the property taken for war purposes has been returned, but there hangs over private enterprise still the menace of seizure, blighting in its effect, paralyzing in its result, to the public detriment. But it matters not whether property can be taken by seizure, or through the process of taxation for extravagant and unnecessary expenditures, there should be an end to both operations. The reason is plain. Ultimately the control of the resources of the people is control of the people. Either the people must own the government or the government will own the people. To sustain a government of the people there must be maintained a property of the people. There can be no political independence without economic independence.

Another source of the gravest public concern has been the reactionary tendency to substitute private will for the public will. Instead of inquiring what the law was and then rendering it full obedience, there has been a disposition on the part of some individuals and of groups to inquire whether they liked the law, and if not, to disregard it, seek to override it, suspend it, and prevent its execution, sometimes by the method of direct action, for the purpose of securing their own selfish ends.

The observance of the law is the greatest solvent of public ills. Men speak of natural rights, but I challenge any one to show where in nature any rights ever existed or were recognized until there was established for their declaration and protection a duly promulgated body of corresponding laws. The march of civilization has been ever under the protecting aegis of the law. It is the strong defense of the weak, the ever-present refuge of innocence, a mighty fortress of the righteous. One with the law is a majority. While the law is observed the progress of civilization will continue. When such observance ceases, chaos and the ancient night of despotism will come again. Liberty goes unsupported or relies in its entirety on the maintenance of order and the execution of the law.

There is yet another manifest disposition which has preyed on the weakness of the race from its infancy, denounced alike by the letter and the spirit of the Constitution, and repugnant to all that is American, the attempt to create class distinctions. In its full development this means the caste system, wherein such civilization as exists is rigidly set, and that elasticity so necessary for progress, and that recognition of equality which has been the aim and glory of our institutions, are destroyed and denied. Society to advance must be not a dead form but a living organism, plastic, inviting progress. There are no classes here. There are different occupations and different stations, certainly there can be no class of employer and employed. All true Americans are working for each other, exchanging the results of the efforts of hand and brain wrought through the unconsumed efforts of yesterday, which we call capital, all paying and being paid by each other, serving and being served. To do otherwise is to stand disgraced and alien to our institutions. This means that government must look at the part in the light of the whole, that legislation must be directed not for private interest but for public welfare, and that thereby alone will each of our citizens find their greatest accomplishment and success.

If the great conflict has disturbed our political conditions it has caused an upheaval in our economic relations. The mounting prices of all sorts of commodities has put a well nigh unbearable burden on every home. Much of this is beyond relief from law, but forces of the government can and must afford a considerable remedy.

The most obvious place to begin retrenching is by eliminating the extravagance of the government itself. In this the Congress has made a commendable beginning, but although the Congress makes the appropriations, the departments make the expenditures which are not under legislative but executive control. The extravagant standards bred of recent years must be eliminated. This should show immediately in reduced taxation. The great breeder of public and private extravagance, the excess profits tax, should be revised and recourse had to customs taxes on imports, one of the most wholesome of all means of raising revenue, for it is voluntary in effect, and taxes consumption rather than production. It should be laid according to the needs of a creditor nation, for the protection of the public, with a purpose to render us both economically and defensively independent.

A revision of taxation must be accompanied with a reduction of that private extravagance which the returns from luxury taxes reveal as surpassing all comprehension. Waiving the moral effect, the economic effect of such extravagance is to withdraw needed capital and labor from essential industries, greatly increasing the public distress and unrest.

There has been profiteering. It should be punished because it is wrong. But it is idle to look to such action for relief. This class profit by scarcity, but they do not cause it.

As every one knows now, the difficulty is caused by a scarcity of material, an abundance of money, and insufficient production. The government must reduce the amount of money as fast as it can without curtailing necessary credits. Production must be increased. All easy to say but difficult of accomplishment.

One of the chief hindrances to production is lack of adequate railroad facilities. Transportation must be re-established. A few glaring instances in the past of improper management joined with an improper public attitude thereby created, wrought great harm to our railroads. Government operation left them disintegrated, disorganized, and demoralized. On their service depends agriculture and industry, the entire public welfare. They must be provided with credit and capital and given the power to serve. This can only be done by removing them from speculation, restoring their prosperity by increased revenues where necessary, thereby re-establishing them in the confidence of the investing public. Their employees must be compensated in accordance with the great importance of the service they render. The whole railroad operation must be restored to public confidence by public support.

There must be a different public attitude toward industry, a larger comprehension of the interdependence of capital, management, and labor, and better facilities for the prompt and reasonable adjustment of industrial disputes. It is well to remember, too, that high prices produce their own remedy under the law of supply and demand. Already in the great leather and woolen industries there is a recession in the basic elements which must soon be reflected in retail prices. When buying stops prices come down.

This condition has borne with especial severity on the agricultural interests of the nation. To cope with it the farmers need an enlarged power of organization whereby the original producer may profit to a larger degree by the high prices paid for his produce by the ultimate consumer, and at the same time decrease the cost of food. The economic strength of a country rests on the farm. Industrial activity is dependent upon it. It replenishes the entire life of the nation. Agriculture is entitled to be suitably rewarded and on its encouragement and success will depend upon the production of a food supply large enough to meet the public needs at reasonable cost.

But all these difficulties depend for final solution on the character and moral force of the nation. Unless these forces abound and manifest themselves in work done there is no real remedy.

There has been a great deal of misconception as to what was won by the victory in France. That victory will not be found to be a substitute for further human effort and endeavor. It did not create magic resources out of which wages could be paid that were not earned, or profits be made without corresponding service, it did not overcome any natural law, it did conquer an artificial thralldom sought to be imposed on mankind and establish for all the earth a new freedom and a larger liberty. But that does not, cannot, mean less responsibility, it means more responsibility, and until the people of this nation understand and accept this increased responsibility and meet it with increased effort there will be no relief from the present economic burdens.

In all things a return to a peace basis does not mean the basis of 1914. That day is gone. It means a peace basis of the present, higher, nobler, because of the sacrifices made and the duties assumed. It is not a retreat, it is a new summons to advance.

Diminishing resources warn us of the necessity of conservation. The public domain is the property of the public. It is held in trust for present and future generations. The material resources of our country are great, very great, but they are not inexhaustible. They are becoming more and more valuable and more and more necessary to the public welfare. It is not wise either to withhold water power, reservoir sites, and mineral deposits from development or to deny a reasonable profit to such operations. But these natural resources are not to be turned over to speculation to the detriment of the public. Such a policy would soon remove these resources from public control and the result would be that soon the people would be paying tribute to private greed. Conservation does not desire to retard development. It permits it and encourages it.

It is a desire honestly to administer the public domain. The time has passed when public franchises and public grants can be used for private speculation.

Whenever in the future this nation undertakes to assess its strength and resources, the largest item will be the roll of those who served her in every patriotic capacity in the world war. There are those who bore the civil tasks of that great undertaking, often at heavy sacrifices, always with the disinterested desire to serve their country. There are those who wore the uniform. The presence of the living, the example of the dead, will ever be a standing guaranty of the stability of our republic. From their rugged virtue springs a never-ending obligation to hold unimpaired the principles established by their victory. Honor is theirs forevermore.

Duty compels that those promises, so freely made, that out of their sacrifices they should have a larger life, be speedily redeemed. Care of dependents, relief from distress, restoration from infirmity, provision for education, honorable preferment in the public service, a helping hand everywhere, are theirs not as a favor but by right. They have conquered the claim to suitable recognition in all things. The nation which forgets its defenders will be itself forgotten.

Our country has a heart as well as a head. It is social as well as individual. It has a broad and extending sympathy. It looks with the deepest concern to the welfare of those whom adversity still holds at the gateways of the all-inclusive American opportunity. Conscious that our resources have now reached a point where there is an abundance for all, we are determined that no imposition shall hereafter restrain the worthy their heritage. There will be, can be, no escape from the obligation of the strong to bear the burdens of civilization, but the weak must be aided to become strong. Ample opportunity for education at public expense, reasonable hours of employment always under sanitary conditions, a fair and always a living wage for faithful work, healthful living conditions, childhood and motherhood, cherished, honored, rescued from the grasp of all selfishness and rededicated to the noblest aspiration of the race, these are not socialistic vagaries but the mark of an advancing American civilization, revealed in larger social justice, tempered with an abounding mercy. In this better appreciation of humanity the war carried the nation forward to a new position, which it is our solemn duty not only to maintain but amplify and extend.

There is especially due to the colored race a more general recognition of their constitutional rights. Tempted with disloyalty they remained loyal, serving in the military forces with distinction, obedient to the draft to the extent of hundreds of thousands, investing $1 out of every $5 they possessed in Liberty Bonds, surely they hold the double title of citizenship, by birth and by conquest, to be relieved from all imposition, to be defended from lynching, and to be freely granted equal opportunities.

Equal suffrage for which I have always voted is coming. It is not a party question, although nearly six-sevenths of the ratifying legislatures have been Republican. The Party stands pledged to use its endeavor to hasten ratification, which I trust will be at once accomplished.

There are many domestic questions which I cannot discuss here, their solution is amply revealed in the platform, such as merchant marine, an adequate army and navy, the establishment of a Department of Public Works, support of the classified civil service laws, provision for public waterways and highways, a budget system and other equally pressing subjects. I am not unmindful of their deep importance.

The foreign relations of our country ought not to be partisan, but American. If restored to the limitations of constitutional authority on the one hand, and to the protection of the constitutional rights of our citizens on the other, much of their present difficulty would disappear.

There can be no sovereignty without a corresponding duty. It is fundamental that each citizen is entitled to the equal protection of the laws. That goes with his citizenship and abides where he lawfully abides, whether at home or abroad. This inherent right must be restored to our people and observed by our government. The persons and property of Americans, wherever they may lawfully be, while lawfully engaged, must forever have protection sufficient to insure their safety and cause the punishment of all who violate it. This is theirs as a plain constitutional duty. A government disregarding it invites the contempt of the world and is on the way to humiliation and war. Rejecting the rule of law is accepting the sword of force.

The country cannot be securely restored to a peace basis in anything until a peace is first made with those with whom we have been at war. The Republicans in Congress, realizing that because of the necessary reliance of one nation on another, there was, more than ever before, mutual need of the sustaining influence of friendly co-operation and rapprochement, twice attempted the establishment of such peace by offers of ratification, which were rejected by the Democratic administration. No one knows now whether war or peace prevails. Our Party stands pledged to make an immediate peace as soon as it is given power by the people.

The proposed League of Nations without reservations as submitted by the President to the Senate met with deserved opposition from the Republican Senators. To a League in that form, subversive of the traditions and the independence of America, the Republican Party is opposed. But our Party by the record of its members in the Senate and by the solemn declaration of its platform, by performance and by promise, approves the principle of agreement, among nations to preserve peace, and pledges itself to the making of such an agreement, preserving American independence, and rights, as will meet every duty America owes to humanity.

This language is purposely broad, not exclusive but inclusive. The Republican Party is not narrow enough to limit itself to one idea, but wise and broad enough to provide for the adoption of the best plan that can be devised at the time of action. The Senate received a concrete proposition, utterly unacceptable without modifications, which the Republican Senators effected by reservations, and so modified twice voted for ratification, which the Democratic administration twice defeated. The platform approves this action of the Senators. The Republicans insisted on reservations which limit. The Democratic platform and record permit only of reservations unessential and explanatory.

We have been taking counsel together concerning the welfare of America. We have spent much time discussing the affairs of government, yet most of the great concourse of people around me hold no public office, expect to hold no public office. Still in solemn truth they are the government, they are America. We shall search in vain in legislative halls, executive mansions, and the chambers of the judiciary for the greatness of the government of our country. We shall behold there but a reflection, not a reality, successful in proportion to its accuracy.

In a free republic a great government is the product of a great people. They will look to themselves rather than government for success.

The destiny, the greatness of America lies around the hearthstone. If thrift and industry are taught there, and the example of self-sacrifice oft appears, if honor abide there, and high ideals, if there the building of fortune be subordinate to the building of character, America will live in security, rejoicing in an abundant prosperity and good government at home, and in peace, respect, and confidence abroad. If these virtues be absent there is no power that can supply these blessings. Look well then to the hearthstone, therein all hope for America lies.

Charter Membership

Secretary HOME TOWN COOLIDGE CLUB, Plymouth, Vermont.

Please enroll me as a Charter member in the Home Town Coolidge Club of Plymouth, Vermont. Send me Membership Certificate, Club Emblem, and Booklet—"Calvin Coolidge—Vermonter."

I enclose membership fee of ($1.00) one dollar.

Name ....

Address ....

....

Calvin Coolidge was born in this town (Plymouth, Vermont) July 4, 1872, and this club is organized by his friends and neighbors for the purpose of promoting his candidacy and election as President.

Inaugural Address of Calvin Coolidge
Washington, D.C.
Wednesday, March 4, 1925

My Countrymen:

No one can contemplate current conditions without finding much that is satisfying and still more that is encouraging. Our own country is leading the world in the general readjustment to the results of the great conflict. Many of its burdens will bear heavily upon us for years, and the secondary and indirect effects we must expect to experience for some time. But we are beginning to comprehend more definitely what course should be pursued, what remedies ought to be applied, what actions should be taken for our deliverance, and are clearly manifesting a determined will faithfully and conscientiously to adopt these methods of relief. Already we have sufficiently rearranged our domestic affairs so that confidence has returned, business has revived, and we appear to be entering an era of prosperity which is gradually reaching into every part of the Nation. Realizing that we can not live unto ourselves alone, we have contributed of our resources and our counsel to the relief of the suffering and the settlement of the disputes among the European nations. Because of what America is and what America has done, a firmer courage, a higher hope, inspires the heart of all humanity.

These results have not occurred by mere chance. They have been secured by a constant and enlightened effort marked by many sacrifices and extending over many generations. We can not continue these brilliant successes in the future, unless we continue to learn from the past. It is necessary to keep the former experiences of our country both at home and abroad continually before us, if we are to have any science of government. If we wish to erect new structures, we must have a definite knowledge of the old foundations. We must realize that human nature is about the most constant thing in the universe and that the essentials of human relationship do not change. We must frequently take our bearings from these fixed stars of our political firmament if we expect to hold a true course. If we examine carefully what we have done, we can determine the more accurately what we can do.

We stand at the opening of the one hundred and fiftieth year since our national consciousness first asserted itself by unmistakable action with an array of force. The old sentiment of detached and dependent colonies disappeared in the new sentiment of a united and independent Nation. Men began to discard the narrow confines of a local charter for the broader opportunities of a national constitution. Under the eternal urge of freedom we became an independent Nation. A little less than 50 years later that freedom and independence were reasserted in the face of all the world, and guarded, supported, and secured by the Monroe Doctrine. The narrow fringe of States along the Atlantic seaboard advanced its frontiers across the hills and plains of an intervening continent until it passed down the golden slope to the Pacific. We made freedom a birthright. We extended our domain over distant islands in order to safeguard our own interests and accepted the consequent obligation to bestow justice and liberty upon less favored peoples. In the defense of our own ideals and in the general cause of liberty we entered the Great War. When victory had been fully secured, we withdrew to our own shores unrecompensed save in the consciousness of duty done.

Throughout all these experiences we have enlarged our freedom, we have strengthened our independence. We have been, and propose to be, more and more American. We believe that we can best serve our own country and most successfully discharge our obligations to humanity by continuing to be openly and candidly, intensely and scrupulously, American. If we have any heritage, it has been that. If we have any destiny, we have found it in that direction.

But if we wish to continue to be distinctively American, we must continue to make that term comprehensive enough to embrace the legitimate desires of a civilized and enlightened people determined in all their relations to pursue a conscientious and religious life. We can not permit ourselves to be narrowed and dwarfed by slogans and phrases. It is not the adjective, but the substantive, which is of real importance. It is not the name of the action, but the result of the action, which is the chief concern. It will be well not to be too much disturbed by the thought of either isolation or entanglement of pacifists and militarists. The physical configuration of the earth has separated us from all of the Old World, but the common brotherhood of man, the highest law of all our being, has united us by inseparable bonds with all humanity. Our country represents nothing but peaceful intentions toward all the earth, but it ought not to fail to maintain such a military force as comports with the dignity and security of a great people. It ought to be a balanced force, intensely modern, capable of defense by sea and land, beneath the surface and in the air. But it should be so conducted that all the world may see in it, not a menace, but an instrument of security and peace.

This Nation believes thoroughly in an honorable peace under which the rights of its citizens are to be everywhere protected. It has never found that the necessary enjoyment of such a peace could be maintained only by a great and threatening array of arms. In common with other nations, it is now more determined than ever to promote peace through friendliness and good will, through mutual understandings and mutual forbearance. We have never practiced the policy of competitive armaments. We have recently committed ourselves by covenants with the other great nations to a limitation of our sea power. As one result of this, our Navy ranks larger, in comparison, than it ever did before. Removing the burden of expense and jealousy, which must always accrue from a keen rivalry, is one of the most effective methods of diminishing that unreasonable hysteria and misunderstanding which are the most potent means of fomenting war. This policy represents a new departure in the world. It is a thought, an ideal, which has led to an entirely new line of action. It will not be easy to maintain. Some never moved from their old positions, some are constantly slipping back to the old ways of thought and the old action of seizing a musket and relying on force. America has taken the lead in this new direction, and that lead America must continue to hold. If we expect others to rely on our fairness and justice we must show that we rely on their fairness and justice.

If we are to judge by past experience, there is much to be hoped for in international relations from frequent conferences and consultations. We have before us the beneficial results of the Washington conference and the various consultations recently held upon European affairs, some of which were in response to our suggestions and in some of which we were active participants. Even the failures can not but be accounted useful and an immeasurable advance over threatened or actual warfare. I am strongly in favor of continuation of this policy, whenever conditions are such that there is even a promise that practical and favorable results might be secured.

In conformity with the principle that a display of reason rather than a threat of force should be the determining factor in the intercourse among nations, we have long advocated the peaceful settlement of disputes by methods of arbitration and have negotiated many treaties to secure that result. The same considerations should lead to our adherence to the Permanent Court of International Justice. Where great principles are involved, where great movements are under way which promise much for the welfare of humanity by reason of the very fact that many other nations have given such movements their actual support, we ought not to withhold our own sanction because of any small and inessential difference, but only upon the ground of the most important and compelling fundamental reasons. We can not barter away our independence or our sovereignty, but we ought to engage in no refinements of logic, no sophistries, and no subterfuges, to argue away the undoubted duty of this country by reason of the might of its numbers, the power of its resources, and its position of leadership in the world, actively and comprehensively to signify its approval and to bear its full share of the responsibility of a candid and disinterested attempt at the establishment of a tribunal for the administration of even-handed justice between nation and nation. The weight of our enormous influence must be cast upon the side of a reign not of force but of law and trial, not by battle but by reason.

We have never any wish to interfere in the political conditions of any other countries. Especially are we determined not to become implicated in the political controversies of the Old World. With a great deal of hesitation, we have responded to appeals for help to maintain order, protect life and property, and establish responsible government in some of the small countries of the Western Hemisphere. Our private citizens have advanced large sums of money to assist in the necessary financing and relief of the Old World. We have not failed, nor shall we fail to respond, whenever necessary to mitigate human suffering and assist in the rehabilitation of distressed nations. These, too, are requirements which must be met by reason of our vast powers and the place we hold in the world.

Some of the best thought of mankind has long been seeking for a formula for permanent peace. Undoubtedly the clarification of the principles of international law would be helpful, and the efforts of scholars to prepare such a work for adoption by the various nations should have our sympathy and support. Much may be hoped for from the earnest studies of those who advocate the outlawing of aggressive war. But all these plans and preparations, these treaties and covenants, will not of themselves be adequate. One of the greatest dangers to peace lies in the economic pressure to which people find themselves subjected. One of the most practical things to be done in the world is to seek arrangements under which such pressure may be removed, so that opportunity may be renewed and hope may be revived. There must be some assurance that effort and endeavor will be followed by success and prosperity. In the making and financing of such adjustments there is not only an opportunity, but a real duty, for America to respond with her counsel and her resources. Conditions must be provided under which people can make a living and work out of their difficulties. But there is another element, more important than all, without which there can not be the slightest hope of a permanent peace. That element lies in the heart of humanity. Unless the desire for peace be cherished there, unless this fundamental and only natural source of brotherly love be cultivated to its highest degree, all artificial efforts will be in vain. Peace will come when there is realization that only under a reign of law, based on righteousness and supported by the religious conviction of the brotherhood of man, can there be any hope of a complete and satisfying life. Parchment will fail, the sword will fail, it is only the spiritual nature of man that can be triumphant.

It seems altogether probable that we can contribute most to these important objects by maintaining our position of political detachment and independence. We are not identified with any Old World interests. This position should be made more and more clear in our relations with all foreign countries. We are at peace with all of them. Our program is never to oppress, but always to assist. But while we do justice to others, we must require that justice be done to us. With us a treaty of peace means peace, and a treaty of amity means amity. We have made great contributions to the settlement of contentious differences in both Europe and Asia. But there is a very definite point beyond which we can not go. We can only help those who help themselves. Mindful of these limitations, the one great duty that stands out requires us to use our enormous powers to trim the balance of the world.

While we can look with a great deal of pleasure upon what we have done abroad, we must remember that our continued success in that direction depends upon what we do at home. Since its very outset, it has been found necessary to conduct our Government by means of political parties. That system would not have survived from generation to generation if it had not been fundamentally sound and provided the best instrumentalities for the most complete expression of the popular will. It is not necessary to claim that it has always worked perfectly. It is enough to know that nothing better has been devised. No one would deny that there should be full and free expression and an opportunity for independence of action within the party. There is no salvation in a narrow and bigoted partisanship. But if there is to be responsible party government, the party label must be something more than a mere device for securing office. Unless those who are elected under the same party designation are willing to assume sufficient responsibility and exhibit sufficient loyalty and coherence, so that they can cooperate with each other in the support of the broad general principles, of the party platform, the election is merely a mockery, no decision is made at the polls, and there is no representation of the popular will. Common honesty and good faith with the people who support a party at the polls require that party, when it enters office, to assume the control of that portion of the Government to which it has been elected. Any other course is bad faith and a violation of the party pledges.

When the country has bestowed its confidence upon a party by making it a majority in the Congress, it has a right to expect such unity of action as will make the party majority an effective instrument of government. This Administration has come into power with a very clear and definite mandate from the people. The expression of the popular will in favor of maintaining our constitutional guarantees was overwhelming and decisive. There was a manifestation of such faith in the integrity of the courts that we can consider that issue rejected for some time to come. Likewise, the policy of public ownership of railroads and certain electric utilities met with unmistakable defeat. The people declared that they wanted their rights to have not a political but a judicial determination, and their independence and freedom continued and supported by having the ownership and control of their property, not in the Government, but in their own hands. As they always do when they have a fair chance, the people demonstrated that they are sound and are determined to have a sound government.

When we turn from what was rejected to inquire what was accepted, the policy that stands out with the greatest clearness is that of economy in public expenditure with reduction and reform of taxation. The principle involved in this effort is that of conservation. The resources of this country are almost beyond computation. No mind can comprehend them. But the cost of our combined governments is likewise almost beyond definition. Not only those who are now making their tax returns, but those who meet the enhanced cost of existence in their monthly bills, know by hard experience what this great burden is and what it does. No matter what others may want, these people want a drastic economy. They are opposed to waste. They know that extravagance lengthens the hours and diminishes the rewards of their labor. I favor the policy of economy, not because I wish to save money, but because I wish to save people. The men and women of this country who toil are the ones who bear the cost of the Government. Every dollar that we carelessly waste means that their life will be so much the more meager. Every dollar that we prudently save means that their life will be so much the more abundant. Economy is idealism in its most practical form.

If extravagance were not reflected in taxation, and through taxation both directly and indirectly injuriously affecting the people, it would not be of so much consequence. The wisest and soundest method of solving our tax problem is through economy. Fortunately, of all the great nations this country is best in a position to adopt that simple remedy. We do not any longer need wartime revenues. The collection of any taxes which are not absolutely required, which do not beyond reasonable doubt contribute to the public welfare, is only a species of legalized larceny. Under this republic the rewards of industry belong to those who earn them. The only constitutional tax is the tax which ministers to public necessity. The property of the country belongs to the people of the country. Their title is absolute. They do not support any privileged class; they do not need to maintain great military forces; they ought not to be burdened with a great array of public employees. They are not required to make any contribution to Government expenditures except that which they voluntarily assess upon themselves through the action of their own representatives. Whenever taxes become burdensome a remedy can be applied by the people; but if they do not act for themselves, no one can be very successful in acting for them.

The time is arriving when we can have further tax reduction, when, unless we wish to hamper the people in their right to earn a living, we must have tax reform. The method of raising revenue ought not to impede the transaction of business; it ought to encourage it. I am opposed to extremely high rates, because they produce little or no revenue, because they are bad for the country, and, finally, because they are wrong. We can not finance the country, we can not improve social conditions, through any system of injustice, even if we attempt to inflict it upon the rich. Those who suffer the most harm will be the poor. This country believes in prosperity. It is absurd to suppose that it is envious of those who are already prosperous. The wise and correct course to follow in taxation and all other economic legislation is not to destroy those who have already secured success but to create conditions under which every one will have a better chance to be successful. The verdict of the country has been given on this question. That verdict stands. We shall do well to heed it.

These questions involve moral issues. We need not concern ourselves much about the rights of property if we will faithfully observe the rights of persons. Under our institutions their rights are supreme. It is not property but the right to hold property, both great and small, which our Constitution guarantees. All owners of property are charged with a service. These rights and duties have been revealed, through the conscience of society, to have a divine sanction. The very stability of our society rests upon production and conservation. For individuals or for governments to waste and squander their resources is to deny these rights and disregard these obligations. The result of economic dissipation to a nation is always moral decay.

These policies of better international understandings, greater economy, and lower taxes have contributed largely to peaceful and prosperous industrial relations. Under the helpful influences of restrictive immigration and a protective tariff, employment is plentiful, the rate of pay is high, and wage earners are in a state of contentment seldom before seen. Our transportation systems have been gradually recovering and have been able to meet all the requirements of the service. Agriculture has been very slow in reviving, but the price of cereals at last indicates that the day of its deliverance is at hand.

We are not without our problems, but our most important problem is not to secure new advantages but to maintain those which we already possess. Our system of government made up of three separate and independent departments, our divided sovereignty composed of Nation and State, the matchless wisdom that is enshrined in our Constitution, all these need constant effort and tireless vigilance for their protection and support.

In a republic the first rule for the guidance of the citizen is obedience to law. Under a despotism the law may be imposed upon the subject. He has no voice in its making, no influence in its administration, it does not represent him. Under a free government the citizen makes his own laws, chooses his own administrators, which do represent him. Those who want their rights respected under the Constitution and the law ought to set the example themselves of observing the Constitution and the law. While there may be those of high intelligence who violate the law at times, the barbarian and the defective always violate it. Those who disregard the rules of society are not exhibiting a superior intelligence, are not promoting freedom and independence, are not following the path of civilization, but are displaying the traits of ignorance, of servitude, of savagery, and treading the way that leads back to the jungle.

The essence of a republic is representative government. Our Congress represents the people and the States. In all legislative affairs it is the natural collaborator with the President. In spite of all the criticism which often falls to its lot, I do not hesitate to say that there is no more independent and effective legislative body in the world. It is, and should be, jealous of its prerogative. I welcome its cooperation, and expect to share with it not only the responsibility, but the credit, for our common effort to secure beneficial legislation.

These are some of the principles which America represents. We have not by any means put them fully into practice, but we have strongly signified our belief in them. The encouraging feature of our country is not that it has reached its destination, but that it has overwhelmingly expressed its determination to proceed in the right direction. It is true that we could, with profit, be less sectional and more national in our thought. It would be well if we could replace much that is only a false and ignorant prejudice with a true and enlightened pride of race. But the last election showed that appeals to class and nationality had little effect. We were all found loyal to a common citizenship. The fundamental precept of liberty is toleration. We can not permit any inquisition either within or without the law or apply any religious test to the holding of office. The mind of America must be forever free.

It is in such contemplations, my fellow countrymen, which are not exhaustive but only representative, that I find ample warrant for satisfaction and encouragement. We should not let the much that is to do obscure the much which has been done. The past and present show faith and hope and courage fully justified. Here stands our country, an example of tranquility at home, a patron of tranquility abroad. Here stands its Government, aware of its might but obedient to its conscience. Here it will continue to stand, seeking peace and prosperity, solicitous for the welfare of the wage earner, promoting enterprise, developing waterways and natural resources, attentive to the intuitive counsel of womanhood, encouraging education, desiring the advancement of religion, supporting the cause of justice and honor among the nations. America seeks no earthly empire built on blood and force. No ambition, no temptation, lures her to thought of foreign dominions. The legions which she sends forth are armed, not with the sword, but with the cross. The higher state to which she seeks the allegiance of all mankind is not of human, but of divine origin. She cherishes no purpose save to merit the favor of Almighty God.

A Calvin Coolidge Timeline

1845 – John Coolidge (father) born at Plymouth, Vt. (Mar. 30)

1846 – Victoria Josephine Moor (mother) born at Plymouth, Vt. (Mar. 14)

1857 – Carrie Athelia Brown (stepmother) born (Jan. 22)

1868 – John Coolidge and Victoria Moor marry at Plymouth, Vt. (May 6)

1872 – Calvin Coolidge born at Plymouth, Vt. (July 4)

1872 – John Coolidge elected to the Vermont Legislature (Aug. 6)

1874 – John Coolidge re-elected to Vermont Legislature

1875 – Abigail Gratia Coolidge (sister) born (April 15)

1875 – Visits Vermont State House in Montpelier (Nov.)

1876 – Moves across road from birthplace to Coolidge homestead

1876 – John Coolidge re-elected to Vermont Legislature

1877 – Enters school at Plymouth (Sept.)

1878 – Death of Calvin Galusha Coolidge (grandfather) (Dec. 15)

1879 – Grace Goodhue (wife) born at Burlington, Vt. (Jan. 3)

1885 – Death of Victoria Moor Coolidge (mother) (March 14)

1886 – Enrolls at Black River Academy, Ludlow, Vt. (Nov.)

1890 – Abigail Gratia Coolidge (sister) dies (March 6)

1890 – Graduates from Black River Academy (May 23)

1891 – Attends Centennial Celebration of Vermont Statehood at Bennington (Aug. 19)

1891 – Col. John Coolidge (father) marries Carrie Athelia Brown (Sept. 9)

1891 – Attends St. Johnsbury Academy, St. Johnsbury, Vt. (Sept.)

1891 – Enters Amherst College (Sept. 17)

1895 – Graduates cum laude from Amherst (June 26)

1895 – Begins "reading" law at Hammond & Field, Northampton, Ma. (Sept. 23)

1895 – Essay wins Gold Medal from Sons of American Revolution (Dec. 13)

1897 – Grace Goodhue graduates from Burlington High School

1897 – Applies for admittance to Massachusetts bar (June 29)

1897 – Admitted to the Massachusetts bar (July 2)

1897 – Appointed to Republican City Committee from Ward Two

1898 – Opens law practice at Northampton's Masonic Block (Feb. 1)

1898 – Attends Republican State Convention as a delegate from Ward Two

1898 – Grace Goodhue enters the University of Vermont (Fall)

1898 – Grace Goodhue initiated into Pi Beta Phi sorority (Nov. 24)

1899 – Elected councilman from Ward Two, Northampton (Dec. 6)

1899 – Becomes counsel to Nototuck Savings Bank

1900 – Appointed Northampton city solicitor (Jan. 18)

1900 – John Coolidge appointed to staff of Vermont Governor William Wallace Stickney (Oct. 14)

1901 – Re-appointed Northampton city solicitor (Jan. 17)

1902 – Grace Goodhue graduates from University of Vermont

1902 – Replaced as Northampton city solicitor (Jan. 16)

1903 – Appointed Clerk of the Courts, Hampshire County (June 4)

1904 – Becomes chairman, Northampton Republican Committee

1904 – Meets Grace Goodhue

1905 – Marries Grace Goodhue (Oct. 4), Burlington, Vt.; takes up residence at Norwood Hotel, Northampton

1905 – Moves to 5 Crescent Street, Northampton

1905 – Defeated for Northampton School Committee (Dec. 5)

1906 – Death of Sarah Almeda Brewer Coolidge (grandmother) at Plymouth, Vt. (Jan. 2)

1906 – Moves to 21 Massasoit Street, Northampton (Aug.)

1906 – John Coolidge (son) born (Sept. 7)

1906 – Elected to the Massachusetts House of Representatives (Nov. 6)

1906 – Re-elected to the Massachusetts House of Representatives (Nov. 7)

1908 – Calvin Coolidge Jr. (son) born (April 13)

1909 – Elected mayor of Northampton (Dec. 7)

1910 – John Coolidge nominated for Vermont State Senate (June)

1910 – John Coolidge elected to Vermont State Senate (Sept.)

1910 – Re-elected mayor of Northampton (Dec. 6)

1911 – Elected to Massachusetts Senate (Nov. 7)

1912 – Appointed Chairman of the Special Legislative Committee on Conciliation (Feb.)

1912 – Grace Coolidge elected Pi Beta Phi Alpha Province Vice President

1912 – Frank Stearns first meets Coolidge (spring)

1912 – Re-elected to State Senate (Nov. 5)

1913 – Re-elected to State Senate (Nov. 4)

1914 – Elected President of the Massachusetts Senate

1914 – Delivers "Have Faith in Massachusetts" speech (Jan. 7)

1915 – Re-elected President of the Senate (Jan. 6)

1915 – Frank Stearns organizes Amherst alumni dinner in support of Coolidge (May 12)

1915 – Grace Coolidge travels to Berkeley for Pi Beta Phi convention (June-July)

1915 – Asks Ralph Hemenway to join his law practice

1915 – Elected Lt.-Governor (Nov. 2)

1916 – Re-elected Lt.-Governor (Nov. 7)

1917 – Re-elected Lt.-Governor (Nov. 6)

1918 – Elected Governor (Nov. 5)

1919 – Inaugurated Governor (Jan. 2)

1919 – Boston Police Strike (Sept. 9-11)

1919 – Telegraphs Samuel Gompers (Sept. 14)

1919 – Re-elected governor (Nov. 4)

1919 – Second inauguration as Governor (Jan. 8)

1920 – Death of Carrie Brown Coolidge (stepmother) (May 18)

1920 – Nominated for vice-presidency (June 12)

1920 – Officially notified of vice-presidential nomination (July 27)

1920 – Death of Coolidge mentor, W. Murray Crane (Oct. 2)

1920 – Elected Vice-President (Nov. 2)

1921 – Inaugurated as Vice-President (Mar. 4)

1921 – Elected life trustee of Amherst College (May 28)

1923 – Sworn in by his father as thirtieth President (Aug. 3)

1923 – First message to Congress; first official presidential speech broadcast on the radio (Dec. 6)

1924 – Congress overrides veto of Veterans Bonus (May 19)

1924 – Signs Immigration Act of 1924 (May 26)

1924 – Signs bill making American Indians U.S. citizens (June 2)

1924 – Addresses Howard University (June 6)

1924 – Nominated for President (June 12)

1924 – Calvin Coolidge Jr. dies (July 7)

1924 – Elected president (Nov. 4)

1924 – Grace Coolidge receives honorary Ll. D. degree from Boston University (Dec. 18)

1925 – Inaugurated president in Washington; Charles Dawes inaugurated vice president (Mar. 4)

1925 – Spends summer at Swampscott, Massachusetts

1926 – Congress passes Revenue Act, reducing income and inheritance taxes (Feb. 26)

1926 – Death of Colonel John Coolidge at Plymouth (Mar. 18)

1926 – Signs the Public Buildings Act, appropriating $60 million (May 25)

1926 – Spends summer at White Pine Camp in Adirondacks (July 7-Sept. 18)

1926 – Proposes tax cut in annual message to Congress (Dec. 7)

1927 – Calls for naval arms limitation (Feb. 10)

1927 – Signs Federal Radio Act, creating Federal Radio Commission (Feb. 23)

1927 – Vetoes McNary-Haugen Farm Relief Bill (Feb. 25)

1927 – Bestows Distinguished Service Cross on Charles Lindbergh (June 11)

1927 – Vacates the White House; moves to 15 Dupont Circle

1927 – Spends summer at State Game Lodge, Custer State Park, South Dakota

1927 – Announces to press, "I do not choose to run" (Aug. 2)

1927 – Dedicates Mount Rushmore (Aug. 10)

1927 – Proposes anti-lynching law and federal Department of Education and Relief (Dec. 6)

1928 – Opens Pan-American Congress at Havana (Jan. 16)

1928 – Again vetoes McNary-Haugen Farm Relief Bill (May 23)

1928 – John Coolidge graduates from Amherst

1928 – Summers on northern Wisconsin's Brule River (June 15-Sept. 10)

1928 – Signs the Pact of Paris, the Kellogg-Briand Pact (Aug. 28)

1928 – Gives "Vermont" speech at Bennington (Sept. 21)

1929 – Ratifies the Kellogg-Briand Pact (Jan. 17)

1929 – Leaves presidency (Mar. 4); returns to Northampton (Mar. 5)

1929 – Becomes president of American Antiquarian Society

1929 – Publishes *The Autobiography of Calvin Coolidge* (May)

1929 – Grace Coolidge receives honorary doctorate from Smith College

1929 – Grace Coolidge publishes the poem "The Open Door" in memory of Calvin Coolidge Jr. (July 7)

1929 – John Coolidge marries Florence Trumbull, daughter of Connecticut Governor John Trumbull. (Sept. 23)

1930 – In Arizona dedicates Coolidge Dam (Mar. 4)

1930 – Moves to The Beeches, 16 Hampton Terrace, Northampton (May 17)

1930 – Grace Coolidge receives honorary doctorate from the University of Vermont (June)

1930 – Begins syndicated newspaper column, "Calvin Coolidge Says" (June 30)

1931 – Grace Coolidge christens the passenger ship, *President Coolidge* (Feb.)

1932 – Serves on National Transportation Committee

1932 – At Madison Square Garden, speaks for Herbert Hoover (Oct. 11)

1932 – Addresses national radio audience from Northampton on behalf of Hoover (Nov. 7)

1933 – Dies at The Beeches, Northampton (Jan. 5)

1933 – Grace Coolidge becomes Chairman of the Board of Clark School for the Deaf; serves until 1952

1956 – John Coolidge donates the Coolidge homestead to the State of Vermont (June 16)

1956 – Calvin Coolidge Memorial Room dedicated at Forbes Library in Northampton; last public appearance of Grace Coolidge (Sept.)

1957 – Grace Coolidge dies at Northampton (July 8)

1960 – Calvin Coolidge Memorial Foundation established

2000 – John Coolidge dies at Plymouth Notch (May 31)

PRESIDENT
COOLIDGE
LEAVING RUTLAND AUG.3-'23

**The Coolidges returning to Washington following his
August 1923 swearing-in at Plymouth Notch.**
(collection of the author)

A Selected
Calvin Coolidge Bibliography

Abels, Jules, *In the Time of Silent Cal*, New York: G. P. Putnam's Sons, 1969.

Bittinger, Cynthia D. *Grace Coolidge: Sudden Star* Hauppauge (NY): Nova Publishers, 2005.

Carpenter, Ernest C., *The Boyhood Days of Calvin Coolidge*, Rutland: The Tuttle Co., 1925.

Coolidge, Calvin. *The Autobiography of Calvin Coolidge*, New York: Cosmopolitan Book Corp., 1929.

Coolidge, Calvin: *Foundations of the Republic: Speeches and Addresses*, New York: Charles Scribner's Sons, 1926.

Coolidge, Calvin, *"Have Faith in Massachusetts;" Speeches and Addresses of Calvin Coolidge*, Boston: Houghton Mifflin, 1919.

Calvin Coolidge, *Law and Order*, Privately Printed, 1920.

Coolidge, Calvin, *The Price of Freedom: Speeches and Addresses*, New York: Charles Scribner's Sons, 1924.

Coolidge, Calvin, *Supplement to the Messages and Papers of the Presidents Covering the Second Administration of Calvin Coolidge March 4, 1925 to March 4, 1929*, New York: Bureau of National Literature.

Curtis, Jane & Will and Frank Lieberman *Return to These Hills: The Vermont Years of Calvin Coolidge*, Woodstock (VT): Curtis-Lieberman, 1985.

Ferrell, Robert H., *Grace Coolidge: The People's Lady in Silent Cal's White House*, Lawrence: University of Kansas Press, 2008.

Ferrell, Robert H., *The Presidency of Calvin Coolidge*, Lawrence: University of Kansas Press, 1988.

Fleser, Arthur L., *A Rhetorical Study of the Speaking of Calvin Coolidge* Lewiston (NY): Edwin Mellen Press, 1990.

Fuess, Claude M., *Calvin Coolidge: The Man from Vermont*, Boston: Little, Brown, 1940.

Fuess, Claude M., *Calvin Coolidge: Twenty Years After*, Worcester: American Antiquarian Society, 1954.

Gilfond, Duff, *The Rise of Saint Calvin: Merry Sidelights on the Career of Mr. Coolidge*, New York: Vanguard, 1932.

Greenberg, David *Calvin Coolidge*, New York: Times Books, 2006.

Greene, J. R., *Calvin Coolidge: A Biography in Picture Postcards*, Vermont, Athol (MA): The Transcript Press, 1987.

Greene, J. R., *Calvin Coolidge's Plymouth, Vermont*, Dover (NH): Arcadia Publishing, 1997.

Hannaford, Peter *The Quotable Calvin Coolidge: Sensible Words for a New Century*, Bennington (VT): Images from the Past, 2001.

Haynes, John Earl (ed.), *Calvin Coolidge and the Coolidge Era*, Washington: The Library of Congress, 1998.

Hogg, Hon. Arthur Prentice, *Calvin Coolidge: Memorial Address delivered Before the Joint meeting of the Two Houses of Congress as a Tribute of Respect to the Late President of the United States*, Washington: United States Government Printing Office, 1933.

Krug, Larry L., *The 1924 Coolidge-Dawes Lincoln Tour* Atglen (PA): Schiffer Books, 2007.

Hoover, Irwin Hood (Ike), *42 Years in the White House*, Boston: Houghton Mifflin Co., 1934.

Lathem, Edward Connery (ed.), *Calvin Coolidge Says: Dispatches Written by Former President Coolidge and Syndicated to Newspapers in 1930-1931*, Plymouth (VT): Calvin Coolidge Memorial Foundation, 1972.

Lathem, Edward Connery (ed.), *Meet Calvin Coolidge: The Man Behind the Myth*, Brattleboro: The Stephen Greene Press, 1960.

Lathem, Edward Connery (ed.), *Your Son, Calvin Coolidge: A Selection of Letters from Calvin Coolidge to His Father*, Montpelier: Vermont Historical Society, 1968.

Lockwood, Allison, *A President in a Two-Family House: Calvin Coolidge of Northampton*, Northampton (MA): Northampton Historical Society, 1988.

McCoy, Donald R., *Calvin Coolidge: The Quiet President*, Lawrence: University Press of Kansas, 1967.

McKee, John Hiram, *Coolidge Wit and Wisdom: 125 Short Stories About "Cal,"* New York: Frederick A. Stokes Co., 1933.

Moore, Herbert Luther, *Calvin Coolidge: From the Farm to the White House*, Rutland: Tuttle Publishing Co., 1935.

National Notary Association, *Why Coolidge Matters: How Civility in Politics Can Bring a Nation Together* Chatsworth (CA): National Notary Association, 2010.

Orton, Vrest, *Calvin Coolidge's Unique Vermont Inauguration*, Plymouth: The Calvin Coolidge Memorial Foundation, 1970.

Quint, Howard H. and Robert H. Ferrell (eds.), *The Talkative President: The Off-The-Record Press Conferences of Calvin Coolidge*, Amherst: University of Massachusetts Press, 1964.

Pietrusza, David *1920: The Year of the Six Presidents*, New York: Carroll & Graf, 2007.

Rogers, Cameron, *The Legend of Calvin Coolidge*, Garden City (NY): Doubleday, Doran & Co., 1928.

Russell, Francis, *A City in Terror: 1919—The Boston Police Strike*, New York: Viking, 1975.

Silver, Thomas B., *Coolidge and the Historians*, Durham: Carolina Academic Press, 1982.

Slemp, C. Bascom (ed.), *The Mind of the President*, Garden City (NY): Doubleday, Page & Co., 1926.

Sobel, Robert, *Coolidge: An American Enigma*, Washington: Regnery, 1998.

Starling, Col. Edmund W. as told to Thomas Sugrue, *Starling of the White House*, Chicago: Peoples Book Club, 1946.

Stern, Sheldon (issue editor), "Calvin Coolidge: Examining the Evidence—A Conference at the John F. Kennedy Library," *The New England Journal of History*, Volume 5, No. 1, Fall 1998.

Stoddard, Gloria May, *Grace & Cal: A Vermont Love Story*, Shelburne (VT): The New England Press, 1989.

Thompson, Robert J. (ed.), *"Adequate Brevity:" Mental Processes of Calvin Coolidge*, Chicago: M. A. Donohue & Company, 1924.

Tucker, Garland S. III, *The High Tide of American Conservatism: Davis, Coolidge, and the 1924 Election* Austin: Emerald Book Co., 2010.

Wallace, Jerry, *Coolidge: The Radio President*, Plymouth Notch: The Calvin Coolidge Memorial Foundation, 2008.

Waterhouse, John Almon, *Calvin Coolidge Meets Charles Edward Garman*, Rutland: Academy Books, 1984.

Wikander, Lawrence E. and Robert H. Ferrell (eds.), *Grace Coolidge: An Autobiography*, Worland (WY): High Plains Publishing Co., 1992.

White, William Allen, *A Puritan in Babylon: The Story of Calvin Coolidge*, New York: Macmillan, 1939.

White, William Allen, *Calvin Coolidge: The Man Who is President*, New York: Macmillan, 1925.

Whiting, Edward Elwell, *Calvin Coolidge: His Ideals of Citizenship*, Boston: Q. A. Wilde Co., 1924.

Woods, Robert A., *The Preparation of Calvin Coolidge: An Interpretation*, Boston: Houghton Mifflin Co., 1924.

A Coolidge Family

Photo Album

Calvin Coolidge
(collection of the author)

Grace Goodhue Coolidge
(collection of the author)

"For almost a quarter of a century she has borne with my infirmities,
and I have rejoiced in her graces."

Calvin Coolidge's Father
Colonel John Coolidge
(1845-1926)
(collection of the author)

"The lines he laid out were true and straight, and the curves regular.
The work he did endured."

**Calvin Coolidge's Mother
Victoria Josephine Moor Coolidge
(1846-1885)**
(collection of the author)

"Whatever was grand and beautiful in form and color attracted her. It seemed as though the rich green tints of the foliage and the blossoms of the flowers came for her in the springtime, and in the autumn, it was for her that the mountain sides were struck with crimson and gold."

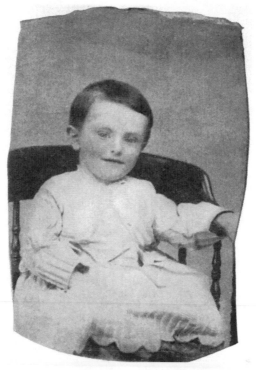

Calvin Coolidge at age three
(collection of the author)

Plymouth Sunday School Picnic, 1887
(Coolidge circled)
(collection of the author)

Plymouth Notch School
(collection of the author)

Calvin Coolidge at age eight
(collection of the author)

Coolidge's class at Black River Academy
(collection of the author)

Black River Academy
(collection of the author)

Coolidge at age seventeen
(collection of the author)

Calvin Coolidge as an Amherst undergraduate
(collection of the author)

**Calvin Coolidge plowing the fields at
Plymouth Notch, Vermont**
(collection of the author)

At Plymouth Notch, Vermont
(collection of the author)

**Calvin Coolidge, Colonel John Coolidge, and
Victoria Moor Coolidge's sister Gratia Moor Wilder**
(collection of the author)

(courtesy of the Library of Congress)

VERMONT BETA—UNIVERSITY OF VERMONT

Grace Goodhue at the University of Vermont
(Pi Beta Phi sorority—third from left, bottom row)
(collection of the author)

Grace Coolidge in 1915
(collection of the author)

"a two-family house"
21 Massasoit Street, Northampton, Massachusetts
(collection of the author)

"So long as I lived there, I could be independent and serve the public without ever thinking that I could not maintain my position if I lost my office."

Northampton City Hall
(collection of the author)

Calvin Coolidge Jr., Grace Coolidge and John Coolidge
(collection of the author)

Calvin Coolidge Jr.
(courtesy of the Library of Congress)

Calvin Coolidge with his sons Calvin Jr. and John
(collection of the author)

Calvin and Grace Coolidge
(collection of the author)

Coolidge advisor
Frank Waterman Stearns
(collection of the author)

"He never obtruded or sought any favor for himself or any other person, but his whole effort was always disinterested and entirely devoted to assisting me when I indicated I wished him to do so. It is doubtful if any other public man ever had so valuable and unselfish a friend."

Troops called in during the Boston Police Strike of 1919
(collection of the author)

HE GIVES AID AND COMFORT TO THE ENEMIES OF SOCIETY.
—McCutcheon in the Chicago *Tribune.*

(collection of the author)

**Governor Calvin Coolidge and
Boston Police Commissioner
Edwin Upton Curtis**
(collection of the author)

"He [Curtis] was also absolutely incorruptible, stubborn on a matter of
principle, and invincibly courageous a very fine type of public servant."

Coolidge Biographer Claude M. Feuss

**The 1920 Republican Convention that stampeded and nominated
Calvin Coolidge as Vice President**
(collection of the author)

Senator Irvine Lenroot
(collection of the author)

1920 Campaign Button
(collection of the author)

**Warren and Florence Harding and
Grace and Calvin Coolidge
at Washington's Union Station**
(collection of the author)

**A Harding-Coolidge
campaign watch fob**
(collection of the author)

1920 Campaign recording
(collection of the author)

**Calvin Coolidge at his official
Vice Presidential Notification Ceremony
Northampton, Massachusetts
July 27, 1920**
(collection of the author)

"Ultimately the control of the resources of the people is control of the people.
Either the people must own the government
or the government will own the people."

Cartoon marking the occasion of Calvin Coolidge's notification in Northampton of his July 27, 1920 vice-presidential nomination.
(collection of the author)

(collection of the author)

An ad for the Harding-Coolidge ticket in the black press
(collection of the author)

(collection of the author)

IT'S A GREAT DAY FOR AMERICA

Columbia —"Congratulations"

Dayton Daily News cartoon congratulating Harding and Coolidge
following their November 1920 landslide
(collection of the author)

The Harding-Coolidge inaugural
(courtesy of the Library of Congress)

The Harding Cabinet
Charles Evans Hughes and Calvin Coolidge sit on either side of Harding.
Herbert Hoover is top right, second from the end.
(collection of the author)

Vice-President Coolidge
exercising in the Congressional gym
(courtesy of the Library of Congress)

Col. John Coolidge at the site of his son's
August 1923 inauguration
(collection of the author)

The Coolidges at Warren Harding's August 1923 funeral
(courtesy of the Library of Congress)

**Newsmen cheering Coolidge following his
first presidential news conference, August 1923**
(courtesy of the Library of Congress)

Photographing the Coolidge Cabinet
Charles Evans Hughes and Andrew Mellon sit alongside Coolidge.
(courtesy of the Library of Congress)

Coolidge in mourning for his son Calvin
(courtesy of the Library of Congress)

Calvin and Grace Coolidge, with members of the
Republican Businessmen's Association of New York in October 1924
(courtesy of the Library of Congress)

Miss Ruth Muskrat of the Cherokee tribe presents Coolidge with a copy of
The Red Man in the United States, a Survey of the Present Day American Indian
at the White House in December 1923
(courtesy of the Library of Congress)

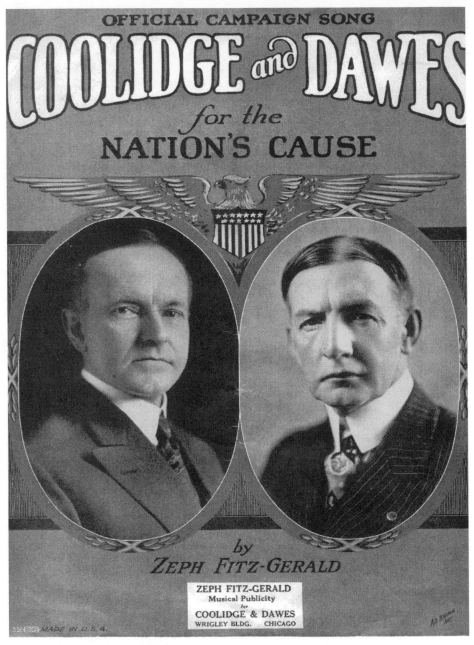

Coolidge-Dawes campaign sheet music
(collection of the author)

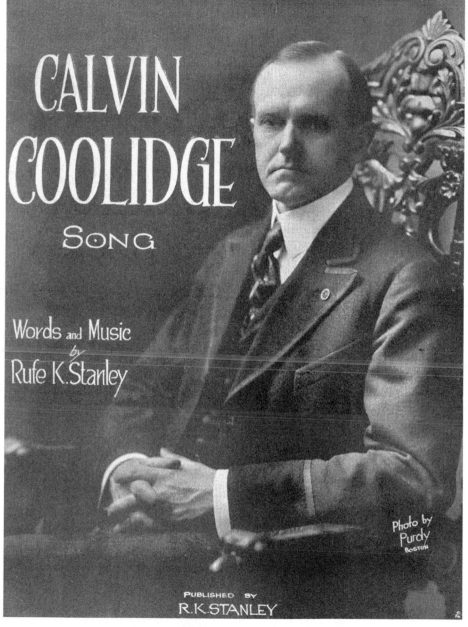

Coolidge 1924 campaign sheet music
(collection of the author)

For Delegate at Large
Republican National Convention

Ralph Beaver Strassburger
Of Montgomery County

For COOLIDGE for PRESIDENT

Your vote and influence
respectfully requested

PRIMARIES, APRIL 22, 1924

*How to vote for Coolidge National
Delegates*   *—See other side*

A 1924 Coolidge delegate from Norristown, Pennsylvania.
(collection of the author)

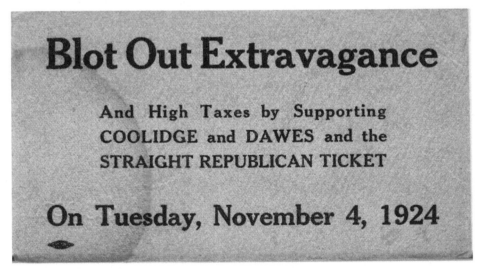

Blot Out Extravagance

And High Taxes by Supporting
COOLIDGE and DAWES and the
STRAIGHT REPUBLICAN TICKET

On Tuesday, November 4, 1924

A Coolidge-Dawes Campaign handout from 1924
(collection of the author)

An ad for the 1924 Michigan GOP ticket
(collection of the author)

En route to his inauguration with Senator Charles Curtis
Both Coolidge and Curtis were of partial American Indian blood.
(courtesy of the Library of Congress)

The March 4, 1925 inaugural motorcade
(courtesy of the Library of Congress)

Sworn in by Chief Justice William Howard Taft on March 4, 1925
(collection of the author)

Signing the Revenue Act, reducing income taxes, February 1926
(courtesy of the Library of Congress)

CALVIN COOLIDGE

"WE ARE THE POSSESSORS OF TRE-
MENDOUS POWER, BOTH AS INDIVIDUALS
AND AS STATES. THE GREAT QUESTION OF
THE PRESERVATION OF OUR INSTITUTIONS IS
A MORAL QUESTION. SHALL WE USE OUR
POWER FOR SELF-AGGRANDIZEMENT OR
FOR SERVICE? IT HAS BEEN THE LACK OF
MORAL FIBRE WHICH HAS BEEN THE DOWN-
FALL OF THE PEOPLES OF THE PAST."

From Calvin Coolidge's Address before the
VERMONT HISTORICAL SOCIETY, January 18, 1921

Photograph by Bachrach   © 1921 Walton Ptg & Prtg Co. Boston, Mass. U.S.A.

(collection of the author)

Grace Coolidge at the April 1925 White House Easter Egg Hunt
(courtesy of the Library of Congress)

**Coolidge decorating Henry Breault of the submarine 0-5
with the Congressional Medal of Honor, October 1924**
(courtesy of the Library of Congress)

Grace Coolidge and her pet raccoon Rebecca
(courtesy of the Library of Congress)

Sent from Peru, Mississippi, Rebecca the raccoon arrived at the White House to be part of a Thanksgiving feast. But the Coolidges found her to be almost entirely domesticated and rather too pleasant to be sautéed.

Coolidge would often play with the raccoon after his afternoon paperwork was done—and as in the case of their cat Tige—stroll about the White House with Rebecca draped around his neck. The majority of the White House staff disliked her (she was always tearing clothes and ripping silk stockings). When Rebecca had scampered up Mrs. Coolidge's social secretary, Mary Randolph, Calvin teased the nervous Miss Randolph: "I think that little coon could bite if she had a mind too."

Although Grace Coolidge was America's first First Lady to achieve a college
degree, she studiously avoided providing any political opinions and,
in photos, was often seen in purely domestic pursuits.
(courtesy of the Library of Congress)

**The Coolidges with Bernard Baruch, throwing out the first ball
for the Washington Senators**
(collection of the author)

**With Washington Senators manager
Stanley "Bucky" Harris at the 1924 World Series**
(courtesy of the Library of Congress)

**Portrait by Howard Chandler Christy of Grace Coolidge
with the family's collie Rob Roy**
(collection of the author)

Calvin Coolidge and labor organizer Mother Jones
(courtesy of the Library of Congress)

President Coolidge dedicating
Washington's Jewish Community Center on May 3, 1925
"The Jewish faith is predominantly the faith of liberty."
(courtesy of the Library of Congress)

SURTAX RATES FOR 1927

Amount of net income	Rate per cent	Surtax	Total surtax on each amount	Amount of net income	Rate per cent	Surtax	Total surtax on each amount
A	B	C	D	A	B	C	D
$10,000				$44,000	11	$440	$2,240
14,000	1	$40	$40	48,000	12	480	2,720
16,000	2	40	80	52,000	13	520	3,240
18,000	3	60	140	56,000	14	560	3,800
20,000	4	80	220	60,000	15	600	4,400
22,000	5	100	320	64,000	16	640	5,040
24,000	6	120	440	70,000	17	1,020	6,060
28,000	7	280	720	80,000	18	1,800	7,860
32,000	8	320	1,040	100,000	19	3,800	11,660
36,000	9	360	1,400	100,000+	20		
40,000	10	400	1,800				

The Income Tax after the Coolidge tax reductions.
(collection of the author)

The swearing in of his secretary Bascom Slemp.
(courtesy of the Library of Congress)

Coolidge being presented with a cowboy outfit in South Dakota
(courtesy of the Library of Congress)

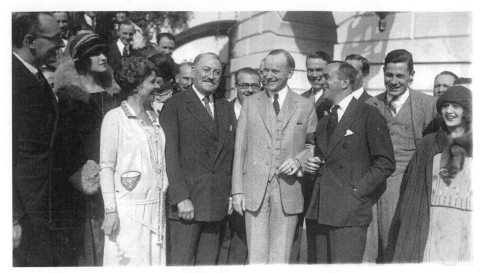

**The Coolidges with John Drew, Al Jolson and other prominent members
of the acting profession in October 1924
(courtesy of the Library of Congress)**

**Groundbreaking for the Hamline Methodist Episcopal Church
(courtesy of the Library of Congress)**

At the Howard University commencement, June 1924
(courtesy of the Library of Congress)

Presenting the Congressional Medal of Honor to Antarctic explorer
Commander Richard E. Byrd USN, February 1927
(courtesy of the Library of Congress)

Coolidge and Helen Keller
(courtesy of the Library of Congress)

**Coolidge and Assistant Secretary of the Navy
Theodore Roosevelt Jr.**
(courtesy of the Library of Congress)

Calvin Coolidge and aviator Charles Lindbergh, June 11, 1927
(collection of the author)

"On behalf of his own people, who have a deep affection for him, and have been thrilled by his splendid achievements, and as President of the United States, I bestow the distinguished Flying Cross, as a symbol of appreciation for what he is and what he has done, upon Colonel Charles A. Lindbergh. Intelligent, industrious, energetic, dependable, purposeful, alert, quick of reaction, serious, deliberate, stable, efficient, kind, modest, congenial, a man of good moral habits and regular in his business transactions."

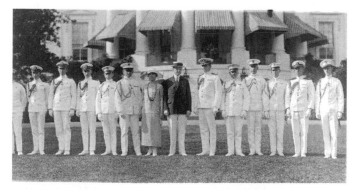

Grace and Calvin Coolidge and their White House aides
(courtesy of the Library of Congress)

"I do not choose to run for President in 1928."
(courtesy of the Library of Congress)

(collection of the author)

**Coolidge and Herbert Hoover at
Hoover's March 4, 1929 inauguration**
(courtesy of the Library of Congress)

A last look at the White House
(courtesy of the Library of Congress)

Calvin Coolidge
Speaks Out

•

It will take you only 6 minutes to read these words of wisdom he uttered in Madison Square Garden, Oct. 11, 1932.

**In October 1932 Coolidge reluctantly spoke out
for Herbert Hoover's ill-fated re-election effort.**

"Before we decide that we want to have a change we ought to determine what the chances are of securing any improvement."
(collection of the author)

Coolidge Grave, Plymouth Notch, Vermont
(collection of the author)

". . . here my dead lie pillowed
on the loving breast of our everlasting hills"